Hong Kong Studies Reader Series

Series Editors
Brian C. H. Fong
Academy of Hong Kong Studies
The Education University of Hong Kong
Tai Po, Hong Kong

Tai-Lok Lui
Academy of Hong Kong Studies
The Education University of Hong Kong
Tai Po, Hong Kong

Stephen Chiu
Academy of Hong Kong Studies
The Education University of Hong Kong
Tai Po, Hong Kong

Hong Kong Studies is an interdisciplinary field of area studies that takes "Hong Kong" as a central subject of analysis.

In recent years, Hong Kong society has undergone significant political, economic and social changes, making Hong Kong Studies the focus of attention for both people inside and outside Hong Kong. As a result, there is a growing demand from local and non-local students, school teachers, scholars, policy researchers, journalists, politicians and businessmen to understand the transformation of Hong Kong in a more systematic way.

The *Hong Kong Studies Reader Series* is designed to address this pressing need. By publishing clear, concise and accessible readers to key areas of Hong Kong Studies ranging from politics and history to society and culture, we aim at offering academic guides to anyone who is interested in understanding and researching Hong Kong.

For Hong Kong Studies, it is probably the best of times.

The Academy of Hong Kong Studies (AHKS), established in July 2015, is the first, and so far only, academy dedicated to fostering Hong Kong Studies within local tertiary institutions. Adopting the strategic direction of "Worlding Hong Kong Studies", the AHKS drives interdisciplinary knowledge creation and transfer initiatives on Hong Kong-centric subjects and fosters the development of a "cross-regional Hong Kong Studies research community".

More information about this series at
http://www.palgrave.com/gp/series/15923

Brian C. H. Fong

Hong Kong Public Budgeting

Historical and Comparative Analyses

palgrave
macmillan

Brian C. H. Fong
Academy of Hong Kong Studies
The Education University of Hong Kong
Tai Po, Hong Kong

The work described in this book was partially supported by a grant from the Research Grants Council of the Hong Kong Special Administrative Region, China (Project No. EdUHK 18600417).

ISSN 2523-7764 ISSN 2523-7772 (electronic)
Hong Kong Studies Reader Series
ISBN 978-981-16-5362-9 ISBN 978-981-16-5363-6 (eBook)
https://doi.org/10.1007/978-981-16-5363-6

This Palgrave Macmillan imprint is published by the registered company Springer Nature Singapore Pte Ltd.
The registered company address is: 152 Beach Road, #21-01/04 Gateway East, Singapore 189721, Singapore

Disclaimer

This book seeks to offer scholarly, descriptive analyses of actors, events, forces, and trends relating to Hong Kong Public Budgeting. It does not express the author's personal, prescriptive view on the constitutional development of Hong Kong. It also does not reflect the official position of The Education University of Hong Kong.

Contents

About the Author

Brian C. H. Fong is an associate professor and associate director of The Academy of Hong Kong Studies at The Education University of Hong Kong. Specialized in great-power competition, democratization, and identity politics, he has produced more than 65 publications including a number of articles in top SSCI journals, including *Democratization*, *Nations and Nationalism*, *Communist and Post-Communist Studies*, *International Public Management Journal*, *International Review of Administrative Sciences*, *The China Quarterly*, *Modern China*, and *Asian Survey*. He is also the founding editor of *Hong Kong Studies Reader Series*, associate editor of *Social Transformation in Chinese Societies*, and first-editor of several comparative politics books including *China's Influence and the Centre-periphery Tug of War in Hong Kong, Taiwan and Indo-Pacific* and *Routledge Handbook of Comparative Territorial Autonomies*.

List of Figures

List of Tables

CHAPTER 1

Introduction

This is a long overdue book. It is long overdue because the last comprehensive, scholarly account of Hong Kong Public Budgeting could be traced back to 1990,[1] which was published 31 years ago even when directly elected seats had not yet been introduced into the Legislative Council and Hong Kong was still a British crown colony.

An update on Hong Kong Public Budgeting is therefore long overdue to account for what has been changed, what has not been changed, and for what reasons. So, this book begins with a basic objective to fill this gap by offering an updated account of Hong Kong Public Budgeting spanning from the pre-1997 British rule to the post-1997 Chinese rule.

[1] There are thus far two major comprehensive, scholarly accounts of Hong Kong Public Budgeting. The first one is Rabushka's *Value for money: The Hong Kong budgetary process* published in 1976 (Rabushka, 1976) and another one is Lo-Cheng Sik-sze's *Public Budgeting in Hong Kong: An Incremental Decision-making Approach* published in 1990 (Lo, 1990). Over the decades, there were dozens of journal articles and book chapters on Hong Kong Public Budgeting (e.g. Cheung, 2005, 2006; Fong, 2015, 2019, 2021a, b; Goodstadt, 2010; Lam, 2002; Scott, 2010: 149–173; Tang, 1997; Wong, 2009), and a few books on specified public budgeting issues such as revenues (Cullen & Wong, 2012) and taxation (Littlewood, 2010). While these studies all have made important contributions to the understanding of different dimensions of Hong Kong Public Budgeting, a book-length study that can serve as an overarching, accessible reader for scholars and students is still missing.

B. C. H. Fong, *Hong Kong Public Budgeting*, Hong Kong Studies Reader Series, https://doi.org/10.1007/978-981-16-5363-6_1

Why Study Hong Kong Public Budgeting

Yet, there are more fundamental theoretical reasons for me to write a comprehensive, scholarly account of Hong Kong Public Budgeting, other than simply providing an updated one. As far as scholarly research is concerned, Hong Kong Public Budgeting must be able to justify its place within the broader literature—a basic but critical issue that we budgeting scholars, researchers, and students from Hong Kong should not be taken for granted.

Public budgeting is fundamentally concerned with "making and implementing decisions regarding the acquisition, allocation and use of resources by government" (Nice, 2002: 2). Public budgeting has often been seen as the single most important function of any government, because it is the lifeblood that sustains all forms of government activities from infrastructural building and public security to social welfare, healthcare, and education (Khan, 2019: vii)—"financial means are the nerves of the states," to use the famous quote of the sixteenth-century French philosopher Jean Bodin.

Given its theoretical significance and practical policy implications, over the decades public budgeting as *a field of study* has been extensively researched by social science scholars worldwide. Against this theoretical backdrop, how should we position Hong Kong as *a research site* relevant to the broader public budgeting studies? To the best of my knowledge, this fundamental theoretical question has never been adequately discussed within the local Hong Kong literature.

My answer to this theoretical question is: Hong Kong Public Budgeting has a great deal to offer to the broader comparative budgeting literature as *a distinctive case of territorial autonomy.*

Broadly speaking, the existing comparative budgeting studies are either central-government focused or symmetric local-government focused, with the former adopting sovereign states as their basic unit of analysis,[2] while the latter using symmetric units of local governments such as cities and states/provinces as their principal units of analysis.[3]

[2] For comparative budgeting studies that focus on sovereign states as the basic unit of analysis, see Lynch & Martin, 1993; Ott, 1993; Guess & Leloup, 2010; Menifield, 2011.

[3] For comparative budgeting studies that adopt symmetric local governments such as cities and states/provinces, see Rubin, 1998; Thurmaier & Willoughby, 2001; Bland, 2007; Shah, 2007; Dollery et al., 2020.

But looking around the world, there are territorial jurisdictions other than sovereign states and symmetric local governments—territorial autonomies have been increasingly set up in different countries to accommodate those demographically distinctive communities; they exercise asymmetric self-government powers, including fiscal autonomy, not available to symmetric local governments within the same countries (Weller & Katherine, 2010). Reading the world map, territorial autonomies could be found across every continent of the globe and their total numbers exceed more than 70 (Ackrén, 2009; Fong & Ichijo, 2022). To name those most prominent examples, that include Aceh (Indonesia), Hong Kong (China), Macao (China), Mindanao (the Philippines), Jammu and Kashmir (India), Jeju Island (South Korea), Sabah (Malaysia), and Sarawak (Malaysia) in Asia, Bougainville (Papua New Guinea), New Caledonia (France), and Norfolk Island (Australia) in the Pacific, Ajaria (Georgia), Gagauzia (Moldova), Gorno-Badakhshan (Tajikistan), and Tatarstan (Russia) in Eurasia, Zanzibar (Tanzania) in Africa, Açores (Portugal), Basques Country (Spain), Catalonia (Spain), Corsica (France), Galicia (Spain), Madeira (Portugal), Northern Ireland (Britain), Scotland (Britain), South Tyrol (Italy), and Wales (Britain) in Europe, Åland Islands (Finland), Greenland (Denmark), and Faroe Islands (Denmark) in the Nordics, Puerto Rico (United States) and Québec (Canada) in the North America.

From the perspective of comparative budgeting, territorial autonomies are a distinctive, hitherto under-researched unit of analysis. Territorial autonomies are distinctive from symmetric local governments such as cities and states/provinces, because they often have special fiscal autonomous powers not available to all other levels of governments within the same country, enabling them to develop their own public budgeting systems from taxation and expenditure to reserve and even currencies and, therefore, to experience a quite different pattern of budgetary politics.[4] Despite their fiscal autonomous powers, most territorial autonomies are not completely fiscally independent,[5] often contesting with their centres

[4] In their survey of 13 territorial autonomies worldwide, Ghai and Woodman (2013) documented the different degrees of fiscal autonomous powers held by Åland, Bosnia-Herzegovina, Bougainville, Catalonia, Hong Kong, Jammu and Kashmir, Macao, Norfolk Island, Puerto Rico, Quebec, Scotland, South Tyrol, and Zanzibar.

[5] Hong Kong and Macao are the two major territorial autonomies that enjoy full-fledged fiscal autonomy, as I will show in the later chapters of this book.

over the scope of their fiscal autonomous powers.[6] The in-betweenness of territorial autonomies vis-à-vis sovereign states and symmetric local governments makes them standing out as a distinctive unit of analysis within comparative budgeting studies, awaiting scholars and researchers to explore. In other words, there is a theoretical imperative to study what makes territorial autonomies typical and what makes them special in the context of public budgeting.

Theoretically speaking, this book endeavours to present Hong Kong Public Budgeting as a case of territorial autonomy. By doing so, I seek to open the window for future comparative budgeting studies across territorial autonomies worldwide.

How to Study Hong Kong Public Budgeting

Public budgeting is multi-dimensional: it is "partly economic, partly political, partly accounting, and partly administrative"—it is an economic instrument that promotes economic growth, a political instrument that allocates resources among competing actors, an accounting instrument that establishes controls over the line-items of government spending, and an administrative instrument that specifies the ways of providing, monitoring, and evaluating public goods and services (Khan, 2019: viii–ix). Owing to its multi-dimensional nature, public budgeting has been studied by social scientists from different disciplines through diversified approaches. Overall, there are three major study approaches in the field, namely managerial, economic, and political (Savage, 2015), each of which focusing on a particular dimension of public budgeting.

Managerial approach focuses on the accounting and administrative dimensions of public budgeting, studying the development of strong systems and best practices for managing government finances. Often using the label of *public financial management*, this study approach principally concerns with "how to do issues" (i.e. what kinds of institutions, systems, and rules should be developed to improve the effectiveness and efficiency of budget execution) rather than "what to do issue" (i.e. should public expenditure be increased or decreased, and should taxation system be adjusted) (Allen et al., 2013: 3). Theoretically, the managerial approach is

[6] A good example in point is Catalonia's ongoing conflicts with Madrid over their "over-contribution" of tax revenues to the centre and "under-allocation" of central resources. See, Castells, 2014.

an outgrowth of the New Public Management (NPM) paradigm, emphasizing on borrowing private sector fiscal management practices, such as performing budgeting, accrual accounting, internal auditing, and so on, to reform the public sector (Allen et al., 2013: 4–5).

Economic approach looks at the economic dimension of public budgeting, studying the role and workings of government in modern market economy. Often carrying the label of *public sector economics* and building on the economic theories of market failure, this study approach develops sophisticated cost-benefit analysis models to examine government budgeting activities (Greene, 2020: 9–31). It also establishes economic forecasting models to analyse public budgeting as fiscal policy tool for managing the macro-economy (Greene, 2020: 37–70).

Political approach examines the political dimension of public budgeting, emphasizing on its nature as a political process featuring the competition of a variety of actors with different priorities (e.g. executive, legislatures, courts, interest groups, press) in different clusters (e.g. the clusters of revenue, expenditure, process, balance, and implementation) (Rubin, 2020). Championed by political scientists and often adopted the notion of *budgetary politics*, this study approach develops different classical political theories to examine the public budgeting process, such as incrementalism, punctuated equilibrium, and rational choice (Savage, 2015).

This book principally adopts the political approach to study Hong Kong Public Budgeting. As a political scientist by training, I have instinctively adopted the political approach when I started to pursue my research agenda on public budgeting a decade ago. The political approach has guided me in the study of different dimensions of Hong Kong Public Budgeting, spanning from institutions and actors to openness, oversight, and allocation. Methodologically, this book can be seen as an attempt to demonstrate how Hong Kong Public Budgeting could be studied from the political approach, offering a guide to both active and future public budgeting researchers who are interested in engaging in such a study approach.

Structure of This Book

The rest of this book will be divided into two major parts.

Part I offers historical analyses on the changed and unchanged of Hong Kong Public Budgeting (Chaps. 2 and 3). Chapter 2 discusses the institutional continuity of the budgetary institutions, including the formation of fiscal conservatism and fiscal autonomy, the codification of such colonial legacies through the 1983 Public Finance Ordinance, and finally their constitutionalization under the 1984 Sino-British Joint Declaration and the 1990 Basic Law. Chapter 3 overviews the changing models of budgetary decision-making, using the transitional period of the 1980–1990s as the dividing line. It firstly examines how the bureaucrats dominated the budgetary decision-making before the 1980–1990s. Then it analyses how the internal and external driving forces, within and outside the Hong Kong government, have transformed the budgetary decision-making since the 1980–1990s.

Part II presents the comparative analyses of Hong Kong Public Budgeting, examining several critical budgeting issues facing the territory (Chaps. 4, 5, and 6). Chapter 4 compares whether and how budget openness in Hong Kong, Macao, and Taiwan is related to their regime trajectories. Chapter 5 compares the budget oversight institutions and practices in Hong Kong and Macao. Chapter 6 examines the dynamics of deficit politics and surplus politics through a comparative analysis of Hong Kong and Singapore. All these comparative analyses aim at firmly placing Hong Kong Public Budgeting within comparative budgeting studies and opening the door for conducting larger scale comparative studies in future.

Finally, the Appendices outline the profiles of Hong Kong Public Budgeting, including the annual budget cycle, the government accounts, the government estimates, glossary of terms, and the financial statistics.

I hope that this book will serve as a theoretically sound, empirically solid, and easily readable guide of Hong Kong Public Budgeting, helping to draw more scholars, researchers, instructors, students, and even policymakers, locally and internationally, into this important but under-studied area. In particular, I hope that this book will help motivate young local scholars to focus on Hong Kong Public Budgeting in their future academic pursuits. Only by doing so, Hong Kong Public Budgeting, as a key area of Hong Kong Studies, will prosper and make its contribution to knowledge.

Further Readings

- Savage, J. D. (2015). Budgeting: Political Science Aspects. In James D. Wright (Ed.), *International Encyclopaedia of the Social & Behavioral Sciences* (2nd ed., pp. 901–905). Oxford: Elsevier.

A good summary of the political approach to public budgeting studies, covering theories such as incrementalism, punctuated equilibrium, and rational choice.

- Rubin, I. (2020). *The Politics of Public Budgeting: Getting and Spending, Borrowing and Balancing* (9th ed.). Thousand Oaks, CA; London: Sage/CQ Press.

One of the most popular texts on the political approach to public budgeting studies, providing a comprehensive summary of different clusters of budgetary politics.

- Ghai, Y. P., & Woodman, S. (2013). *Practising Self-Government: A Comparative Study of Autonomous Regions.* Cambridge, NY: Cambridge University Press.

A classical comparative survey of the constitutional arrangements of territorial autonomies, including their fiscal autonomy. It covers the cases of Åland, Bosnia-Herzegovina, Bougainville, Catalonia, Hong Kong, Jammu and Kashmir, Macao, Norfolk Island, Puerto Rico, Quebec, Scotland, South Tyrol, and Zanzibar. While the comparative survey is law-oriented and is very brief in respect of details, it offers thus far the best starting point for exploring future comparative budgeting studies at territorial autonomies level.

Bibliography

Ackrén, M. (2009). *Conditions for Different Autonomy Regimes in the World: A Fuzzy-Set Application.* Åbo Akademi University Press.

Allen, R., Hemming, R., & Potter, B. H. (2013). Introduction: The Meaning, Content and Objectives of Public Financial Management. In R. Allen, R. Hemming, & B. H. Potter (Eds.), *The International Handbook of Public Financial Management* (pp. 1–12). Palgrave Macmillan.

Bland, R. (2007). *A Budgeting Guide for Local Government.* ICMA Press.

Castells, A. (2014). Catalonia and Spain at the Crossroads: Financial and Economic Aspects. *Oxford Review of Economic Policy, 30*(2), 277–296.

Cheung, A. B. L. (2005). *Budgeting for Results or Budgeting for Politics: Budget Reforms, Fiscal Stability and Distributional Politics in Hong Kong Re-Examineds.* A Paper Presented in the 61st Congress of the International Institute of Public Finance Jeju, Korea, 22–25 August 2005.

Cheung, A. B. L. (2006). Budgetary Reforms in Two City States: Impact on the Central Budget Agency in Hong Kong and Singapore. *International Review of Administrative Sciences, 72*(3), 341–361.

Cullen, R., & Wong, A. (2012). *The Foundations of the Hong Kong Revenue Regime.* Civic Exchange.

Dollery, B., Kitchen, H., Mcmillan, M., & Shah, A. (2020). *Local Public, Fiscal and Financial Governance an International Perspective.* Palgrave Macmillan.

Fong, B. C. H. (2015). The Politics of Budget Surpluses: The Case of China's HKSAR. *International Review of Administrative Sciences, 81*(1), 134–157.

Fong, B. C. H. (2019). Democratization and Budget Openness: Evidences from Hong Kong, Macao, and Taiwan. *International Review of Administrative Sciences.* Article First Published Online: 8 July 2019. https://doi.org/10.1177/0020852319845453

Fong, B. C. H. (2021a). Deficit Politics and Surplus Politics: A Comparative Study of Hong Kong and Singapore. *International Public Management Journal.* Article First Published Online: 1 April 2021. https://doi.org/10.1080/10967494.2021.1903633

Fong, B. C. H. (2021b). Budget Oversight in Territorial Autonomies: A Comparative Analysis of Hong Kong and Macao. *International Review of Administrative Sciences.*

Fong, B. C. H., & Ichijo, A. (2022). *Routledge Handbook of Comparative Territorial Autonomies.* Routledge. [Forthcoming].

Ghai, Y. P., & Woodman, S. (2013). *Practising Self-Government: A Comparative Study of Autonomous Regions.* Cambridge University Press.

Goodstadt, L. F. (2010). Fiscal Freedom and the Making of Hong Kong's Capitalist Society. *China Information, 24*(3), 273–294.

Greene, J. E. (2020). *Public Finance: An International Perspective.* Singapore: World Scientific Publishing Co.

Guess, G., & Leloup, L. (2010). *Comparative Public Budgeting: Global Perspectives on Taxing and Spending.* State University of New York Press.

Khan, A. (2019). *Fundamentals of Public Budgeting and Finance.* Springer Nature.

Lam, J. (2002). Globalization and Fiscal Management in Hong Kong. *New Zealand Journal of Asian Studies, 4*(1), 62–83.

Littlewood, M. (2010). *Taxation Without Representation: The History of Hong Kong's Troublingly Successful Tax System.* Hong Kong University Press.

Lo, C. S. S. (1990). *Public Budgeting in Hong Kong: An Incremental Decision-Making Approach*. Writers' and Publishers' Cooperative.
Lynch, T. D., & Martin, L. (1993). *Handbook of Comparative Public Budgeting and Financial Management*. Marcel Dekker.
Menifield, C. (2011). *Comparative Public Budgeting: A Global Perspective*. Jones & Bartlett Learning.
Nice, D. (2002). *Public Budgeting*. Wadsworth.
Ott, A. (1993). *Public Sector Budgets: A Comparative Study*. E. Elgar Pub.
Rabushka, A. (1976). *Value for Money: The Hong Kong Budgetary Process*. Hoover Institution Press.
Rubin, I. (1998). *Class, Tax, and Power Municipal Budgeting in the United States*. Chatham House.
Rubin, I. (2020). *The Politics of Public Budgeting: Getting and Spending, Borrowing and Balancing* (9th ed.). Sage/CQ Press.
Savage, J. D. (2015). Budgeting: Political Science Aspects. In J. D. Wright (Ed.), *International Encyclopaedia of the Social & Behavioral Sciences* (2nd ed., pp. 901–905). Elsevier.
Scott, I. (2010). *The Public Sector in Hong Kong*. Hong Kong University Press.
Shah, A. (2007). *Local Budgeting*. World Bank.
Tang, S. H. (1997). Budgetary Guidelines and Fiscal Performance in Hong Kong. *International Journal of Public Sector Management, 10*(7), 547–571.
Thurmaier, K., & Willoughby, K. (2001). *Policy and Politics in State Budgeting*. M.E. Sharpe.
Weller, M., & Katherine, N. (Eds.). (2010). *Asymmetric Autonomy and the Settlement of Ethnic Conflicts*. University of Pennsylvania Press.
Wong, W. (2009). The Days After the End of the Asian Miracle: The Budget Crisis of Hong Kong. In S. Ming (Ed.), *Politics and Government in Hong Kong: Crisis Under Chinese Sovereignty* (pp. 136–161). Routledge.

PART I

Historical Analyses

CHAPTER 2

Budgetary Institutions

Public budgets are record of revenues, expenditures, reserves, and debts of a government, indicating what the government intends to do in future and how it is going to finance such activities (von Hagen, 2007). In this regard, *budgetary institutions* are the formal and informal rules, principles, procedures, and arrangements that govern the drafting, adoption, execution, and evaluation of public budgets (Imbeau & Pétry, 2004; Raudla, 2014). The importance of budgetary institutions lies in its impact on setting the scene for the interaction of different budgetary actors in the budgetary process (Hallerberg et al., 2009).

This chapter adopts a historical perspective to trace the formation, codification, and constitutionalization of the two major pillars of the budgetary institutions in Hong Kong, that is the *fiscal conservatism* and the *fiscal autonomy*. The historical analyses will demonstrate the high degree of institutional continuity of Hong Kong's budgetary institutions, which have remained intact throughout both the pre-1997 British rule and the post-1997 Chinese rule, whether it is called British Hong Kong or the China's Hong Kong Special Administrative Region (HKSAR).

B. C. H. Fong, *Hong Kong Public Budgeting*, Hong Kong Studies Reader Series, https://doi.org/10.1007/978-981-16-5363-6_2

Formation of the Colonial Budgetary Institutions

Fiscal Conservatism

If one had to name a basic feature of Hong Kong budgetary institutions, one would probably immediately think of fiscal conservatism, or the "prudent financial management," to use the official jargon of the Hong Kong government (Finance Branch, 1995). Still strongly influencing the budgetary thinking and practice of government officials today, fiscal conservatism is the fundamental rule that guides, regulates, and constrains the formulation of annual budgets and therefore forms the very foundation of Hong Kong's budgetary institutions (Scott, 2010: 152). What does fiscal conservatism mean? Why was it establish in colonial time?

Reading through the history of Hong Kong, fiscal conservatism is a colonial legacy that passes from the pre-1997 British rule to the post-1997 Chinese rule. It can only be fully understood in the historical context of Hong Kong's colonial past. Looking back, fiscal conservatism could be interpreted as an amalgam of both the British Empire and the local government-business alliance, as this chapter will demonstrate.

The fiscal conservatism was primarily inherited from the workings of the British Empire. A major hallmark of the British Empire from the eighteenth to the twentieth century was to "run the Empire on the cheap" (Brendon, 2007: 334). All empires were costly to run, because they unavoidably involved the maintenance and deployment of expensive military forces, especially for the British who built and governed an "empire on which the sun never sets," which spanned across every continent of the globe. Therefore, the fiscal orthodoxy of the British was always to run the empire on the cheap, particularly after the First World War when the signs of strain of the empire had become increasingly apparent (Marquand, 2008: 88). Consequently, on the one hand London had made every effort to control the military cost by requesting all colonies to pay for their own self-defence (Schmitt, 2006: 2–3); while on the other hand it had also put in place an *empire-wide fiscal oversight system* to promote the self-financing of the colonies, trying to prevent colonies from creating any financial burden on the Exchequer (Levine, 2013: 65 and 109; Jansen et al., 2017: 121).

Under this empire-wide fiscal oversight system, London had imposed stringent fiscal disciplines over the spending of its colonies worldwide (Gardner & Roy, 2020: 99) and British Hong Kong was, obviously, no exemption to such controls. In practice, the Colonial Office in London was the principal agency responsible for enforcing the empire-wide fiscal oversight controls over Hong Kong and other British colonies in accordance with the requirements of the *Colonial Regulations* (Rabushka, 1976: 3). Officially titled the *Rules and Regulations for Her Majesty's Colonial Service*, the Colonial Regulations had been firstly introduced into all British colonies in 1837 and was revised periodically thereafter. For this purpose, Hong Kong was for the first time listed under the 1843 version of the Colonial Regulations (Rabushka, 1976: 15). The Colonial Regulations explicitly held the Hong Kong Governor fiscally accountable to the Secretary of State for the Colonies in London, who was empowered to exercise extensive oversight powers including the approval of the annual budgets before the beginning of the fiscal years, the scrutiny of variations in approved estimates, the endorsement of the alteration of salaries of civil servants, the inspection of audited accounts, and so forth (Rabushka, 1976: 15–22). All such oversight controls were practically operated through a specified set of "financial and other returns" that all colonies including the British Hong Kong were instructed under the Colonial Regulations to regularly submit to London (Table 2.1). On top of this empire-wide fiscal oversight system, there was an additional rule that Treasury control would be imposed on those colonies that were receiving subventions from London, such a control would last until the borrowings had been completely paid off (Goodstadt, 2010).

Consequently, London's empire-wide fiscal oversight system, which was operational until the granting of fiscal autonomy in 1958, had built in a strong sense of fiscal conservatism into the public budgeting institutions of Hong Kong from day one. It made stringent fiscal disciplines, including balanced budgets, accumulation of reserves, and avoidance of public debts the greatest mottos of the Hong Kong government officials since the founding of the colony (Rabushka, 1976: 4; Lo, 1990: 40–41).

But the fiscal conservatism should not only be seen as unilaterally imposed by London, but it was also upheld by the local government-business alliance. British Hong Kong was a typical crown colony, under which the all-powerful Governors appointed by London functioned like an absolute monarch performing multiple roles as the head of the government, chairman of the Legislative Council, and the commander-in-chief of the British garrisons (Miners, 1998: 69). While granted extensive constitutional powers under the *Letters Patent* and the *Royal Instructions*, in practice the British Governors relied on a coalition between colonial bureaucrats and business tycoons to maintain effective governance.

Table 2.1 Extracts from the 1843 colonial regulations on submission of financial returns by colonies

Section	*Extracts*
Foreword	"Her Majesty's Government attach the highest importance to the regular and punctual transmission of the following RETURNS; and Governors are desired to impress upon those officers, whose duty it may be to prepare them, that any remissness or neglect, in this respect, will be visited with the marked displeasure of Her Majesty's Government." (Colonial Office, 1843: 52)
I. Returns relating to colonial revenues and receipts	"1. A Return of the regular revenue, arising from local taxes and duties, in which is to be distinguished the amount of collections under each head, and the arrears of preceding years from the receipts of the current year. 2. Of the revenue derived from rents or other proceeds of Crown property. 3. Of causal revenue and incidental receipts, including judicial fines and forfeitures, escheats, and other similar droits of the Crown, and recoveries of debts from individuals. 4. Of repayments of colonial advances, or other receipts on account of that description. 5. Of receipts in aid of revenue, including loans raised, drafts on account of Parliamentary Grants, or other advances from the funds of this country, issues of paper currency, and deposits from the courts of law, or otherwise, which may be for a time available for the purposes of the Colonial government. 6. Of deposit not so available." (Colonial Office, 1843: 52–53)
II. Returns relating to disbursements	"1. A Return of civil charges regularly by Her Majesty's Government, or by Acts of local Legislatures, which have received Her Majesty's assent, classed under the heads of salaries, and of incidental and contingent charges, specifying the amount expended under each head for each public department, including judicial and ecclesiastical establishment paid by the Government. 2. Of supplementary civil charges, comprising any salaries or contingent charges which may not have been regularly sanctioned by Her Majesty's Government, specifying the department and service for which they may have been incurred, and whether such sanction has been applied for. 3. Of military charges, if defrayed from Colonial funds, and not paid by officers accounting to the military departments in this country, under the heads of regimental pay and subsistence of local corps or militia. 4. Of advances for the Colonial service (to be subsequently repaid or accounted for to the Colonial authorities), including remittances to agents.

5. Of advances from the Colonial funds to the military chests, or otherwise, for services to be accounted for by the officers to whom the advances are made to their respective departments in this country.
6. Of repayment of loans, or advances in aid of revenue, and payments for interest thereon, paper currency cancelled, or other debts liquidated.
7. Of repayments of deposits.
8. Of special and particular services, not attaching to the ordinary Colonial establishments, such as Indian presents, the expenditure for liberated Africans in Sierra Leone and in the West Indies, and in the cases of New South Wales, Van Diemen's Land, and Bermuda, the charges for the maintenance, clothing, and lodging the convicts, and for establishments connected with their immediate superintendence and management; any sums received for their labour being stated by way of deduction from the gross amount of the expenditure.
9. Adverting to the variations in the charges defrayed from revenues at the disposal of the Colonial governments, comprising in some instances expenses of a public nature, which, in others, are provided for by separate and special rates, not levied or accounted for by the officers of government, it would be desirable to receive the best returns that can be obtained of the produce and appropriation of all such dues or tolls as are levied or applied by local municipal bodies, or officers, or as may have been imposed by law for any specific purposes, including legislative provision for ecclesiastical, scholastic, or charitable establishments.
10. These several returns and statements should be made out and furnished *quarterly*, and they should comprise not only the revenue and expenditure, and other financial transactions of those Colonies of which the revenues are at the immediate disposal of the Crown but also of those Colonies where the revenues are appropriated by, and accounted for to, Representative Assemblies.
11. The quarterly returns, in those cases where the revenues are at the disposal of the Crown, should be accompanied by a short abstract of the transactions of the treasurer, or other officer accountable to the Lords Commissioners of the Treasury, for the application of the Colonial funds, showing the amount of his receipts and disbursements during the corresponding period, and the balances in hand, or available, at the commencement and end of its.

(*continued*)

Table 2.1 (continued)

Section	*Extracts*
	12. Although the Lords of the Treasury consider that it is very desirable to obtain these returns and statements *quarterly*, they are aware that, in some cases, the Colonial financial returns are made up *annually*, and that it may be difficult to obtain them more frequently, than once in each year; their Lordships would wish, however, to obtain them *quarterly* in all practicable cases. 13. The accounts of revenue and expenditure, of the preceding year, must be transmitted to this country, for examination and audit, on or before the 1st of April in each year. 14. The salary of the Treasurer, or other proper officer, must not be issued to him, until he has certified to the Governor that he has compiled with his instructions. 15. The Auditor will transmit through the Governor such reports as he may from time to time have to make to the Audit Board, in order that the Governor may have an opportunity of adding any explanations which he may judge necessary, thus saving in many cases the necessity of a further reference to the colony. 16. All accounts of expenditure of public money must be accompanied by authenticated copies of, or extracts from, such of the Secretary of State's despatches, as may be referred to in the accounts, in support of particular items of expenditure. 17. A quarterly return or schedule of all appointments to public offices, and of all alterations made in the salaries or allowances of public officers, as also of all payments of an unusual and special description directed or sanctioned by the Governor or officer commanding, should be made out in the forms prescribed in the Appendix, but the Governor must not regard the mere transmission of this return as relieving him from further responsibility." (Colonial Office, 1843: 53–56)
III. Other periodical returns	"1. Copies of the Minutes of the Proceedings of the Houses of Assembly and of the Boards of Privy and Legislative Councils, with an index of the most material contents, and marginal abstracts of the same in each page. 2. Lists of members of Executive and Legislative Councils, specifying the date of their appointment, and whether they hold any other office in the Colony. 3. The Governor will send home two manuscript copies of all Acts passed during the session of the Colonial Legislature. In those Colonies, in which it is customary to print the laws, not fewer than six copies are to be sent; two of which are required for the use of the two Houses of Parliament; and Her Majesty's Government will send out annually to the respective Governors, for the use of the Colonial Legislatures and Courts of Justice, copies of the British statutes, which must be carefully preserved.

4. Whenever a new compilation or corrected edition of the Colonial laws shall be published, four copies are to be forwarded to the Secretary of State; two of which are required for the use of the two Houses of Parliament.
5. A return for the preceding year of all retired allowances upon abolition and reduction of office, specifying the total amount at the beginning of the year; the diminution occasioned by death or otherwise; the addition made during the past year; the age and length of service of each party so added; and the saving of establishment which shall have been made in each such case.
6. A return of all officers whose duties are executed by deputy, and of all officers absent upon leave; with the date from which their leave commenced, and to which it extends.
7. A list of the names of all persons to whom any salaries shall be granted, as stipendiary magistrates, specifying the date of every such commission, and the amount of salary assigned to every such justice of the peace.
8. In consequence of the frequent changes which occur in the appointments of Stipendiary Magistrates, the Secretary of State desires to be furnished likewise with quarterly lists of those in actual employment, specifying the date of appointment and amount of salary, and whether the appointment is or is not provisional.
9. Reports of progress in geographical and topographical knowledge, comprising detailed information on the following points:—First. Accounts of any journeys of discovery into the interior. Second. The division of counties or districts. Third. The construction of canals and roads. Fourth. Latitude and longitude of the sites chosen for establishment of new villages or towns. Fifth. The course of rivers. Sixth. The height of mountains, and, generally, on all such points as may be useful and interesting to science.
10. The reports must be accompanied by such maps and surveys as may be necessary for their elucidation; and the surveyor-general must be called upon, once at least in each year, to report on the progress of his department.
11. Two copies of the Colonial *Book Almanack* for the current year; and copies of Government Gazettes, and generally of such books or pamphlets issuing from the Colonial press as may be useful to this department."
(Colonial Office, 1843: 57–59)

(*continued*)

Table 2.1 (continued)

Section	*Extracts*
IV. The annual "blue book"	"1. The annual "Blue Book," containing specific accounts of the Civil Establishments, of the Colonial Revenue and Expenditure, and of various statistical particulars, &c., must be completed as early as possible after the close of each year. The various returns which it comprises must be filled up with the greatest possible accuracy; and the statistical Tables must be full and complete. Blank copies of this book in sheets will be annually transmitted to each Colony from the Colonial Office. 2. The Colonial Secretary will be responsible for the general preparation of the "Blue Book," and he must certify the accuracy of its contents. 3. The Governor will not be authorized to sign a warrant for payment of the first quarter's salary in each year, which may be otherwise due to the Colonial Secretary, unless he shall have produced a complete Book properly filled up, or can show to the Governor that he has duly called upon the chief officer of the department, in which any delay may have occurred, for the returns required from him. 4. In this case the latter officer must be held responsible for the delay, and payment of his salary must be suspended, until he has forwarded the necessary returns to the Colonial Secretary. 5. The Governor will send home the "Blue Book" in duplicate. He will retain one copy for the use of the Executive Government, and in the Legislative Colonies he will lay a copy of it before the Council and the House of Assembly respectively. 6. The Governor, in transmitting the "Blue Book" to this department, will accompany it with a report exhibiting generally the past and present state of the Colony, and its prospects, in every political branch." (Colonial Office, 1843: 59–60)

Source: Quoted from "Chapter VII: Financial and Other Returns" of the Colonial Regulations (Colonial Office, 1843: 52–60)

Controlling vast economic resources and social networks, the British, European, and local Chinese merchants had several times joined hands to demand a share in government power in the latter half of the nineteenth century and confronted with the Hong Kong government on its various initiatives on taxations and expenditures. The conflicts between the bureaucrats and the capitalists dominated the politics of British Hong Kong for several decades, including their conflicts over the introduction of poll tax and general rates in 1845, imposition of the stamp duty to cover British military expenditure in Hong Kong in 1864, charging from London on British garrisons stationed in Hong Kong in 1890, and the abolition of the Department of Registrar General and reduction of civil service salaries in 1892, to name just a few examples (Scott, 1989: 57–58). After another direct clash between the bureaucrats and the capitalists in 1894, London finally stepped in and agreed to institutionalize the representation of business interests in the colonial political establishment through appointing their representatives as unofficial members of the Executive Council, Legislative Council, and advisory bodies. This marked the beginning of the formation of a stable British-centred government-business alliance in Hong Kong, which almost lasted until end of the British rule in the 1990s (Fong, 2014: 80–81).[1]

One of the implications of the operation of such a stable government-business alliance throughout the twentieth century was the entrenchment of the fiscal conservatism of the Hong Kong government. Considering that any provision of government subsidies to its business allies might attract public backlash, the Hong Kong government walked a fine line by adopting a policy of non-interventionism—trying to accommodate business interests by practicing small government, maintaining a low tax policy, imposing minimal business regulations, and delaying social welfare provisions, so that the capitalists could enjoy a general pro-business policy environment, despite falling short of direct government aids (Goodstadt, 2010). Under the prevalence of the government-business alliance, the business sector had continuously functioned as a watchdog of government spending and taxation (Scott, 1989: 73 and 155), helping to entrench the fiscal conservatism initially imposed by London and to extend it well beyond the granting of full fiscal autonomy in 1958—because the stringent fiscal disciplines were seen by the governing elites as providing "a good set of rules for financial integrity" (Rabushka, 1979: 35).

[1] For an account of the operation of the government-business alliance in British Hong Kong, see Fong, 2015: 73–102.

Fiscal Autonomy

Fiscal autonomy means the devolved authority exercised by local governments in deciding and appropriating budgetary resources on their own, the degree of which always varies widely across countries (Drummond & Mansoor, 2002). Having strong implications on the distribution of powers, responsibilities, and resources between different levels of governments within a country, fiscal autonomy is a critical, controversial issue in modern public budgeting (Pola, 2016) and it has been measured by different comparative scholars through different indicators.[2]

For the British Hong Kong, it had gradually established its full fiscal autonomy from London in the post-war years. Owing to its success in achieving self-financing, Treasury control over the Hong Kong colony had been long relinquished dating back to 1870 and thereafter only Colonial Office's fiscal controls were operational in the territory according to Colonial Regulations (Rabushka, 1976: 34). In the aftermath of the Second World War, Treasury control had been re-imposed, but it was quickly removed again in 1948 due to the strong recovery of the budgetary position of the Hong Kong government (Tang, 1993). Since then, the Hong Kong government kept improving its budgetary position and used it as a bargaining chip to press London for getting rid of the empire-wide fiscal oversights imposed on Hong Kong under the Colonial Regulations (Goodstadt, 2010).

Finally, the historical moment came when Governor Sir Robert Black announced in his annual address to the Legislative Council on 6 March 1958 that London had granted Hong Kong full fiscal autonomy (Rabushka, 1976: 33):

> Before concluding, I have to report a decision recently taken by the Secretary of State. He has approved a considerable relaxation in the financial control which he exercises over Hong Kong. In 1948 the Colony was released from Treasury control and given a large measure of autonomy over its own finances. The control which the Secretary of State still retained at that time was that his approval was still required for the annual Estimates, for supple-

[2] For example, Hooghe et al. (2016: 30) measured fiscal autonomy of a local government according to the extent to which it can independently tax its population and to borrow; Blöchliger (2005) measured fiscal autonomy based on the local governments' share of tax revenue, their discretion over those taxes, their share of transfers, their rights to run deficits, their rights to borrow, and so forth.

> mentary provisions exceeding $1 million in the case of capital expenditure, and for the issue of any loan and for any expenditure involving important points of principle. The Secretary of State has now informed me that, in view of the good standing, financial and administrative, of the Colony, he will further relax his control and will no longer require the Estimates to be submitted for his approval; nor will he require supplementary provisions to be authorized by him. (Quoted from Rabushka, 1976: 34)

The historical granting of full fiscal autonomy to Hong Kong should be interpreted in a broader context of London's informal devolution of powers from the 1950s to the 1970s. The post-war period was the heydays of de-colonialization, through which different European Empires including the British Empire had been simultaneously disintegrated and more than a hundred of colonies became either self-governing dominions or independent sovereign states (Jansen et al., 2017: 1; Levine, 2013: 206–233). Hong Kong was an anomaly in this global process of de-colonialization. Because China was cautious of any attempt to perpetuate Western dominance in Hong Kong, it opposed Britain's plan to transform the territory into a self-governing dominion (Share, 2007: 136). Consequently, Hong Kong had gone through an extraordinary form of de-colonialization, through which a wide range of autonomous powers were informally devolved—not only fiscal autonomy (1958), but also the monetary power to decide on the exchange rate of Hong Kong dollars (1967), the financial power to manage its own foreign exchange reserves (1972), and the external affairs powers to conduct trade negotiations and to join international organizations (1970s) (Goodstadt, 2009: 49–70).

In other words, the granting of fiscal autonomy by London in 1958 was not an isolated incident, it was actually part of the historical process of the formation of Hong Kong's de facto autonomy during the de-colonialization period of the 1950s to 1970s. Yet, it was important to note that British Hong Kong's autonomy, including its fiscal autonomous powers, was fundamentally a system of *undemocratic autonomy* where autonomous powers were exercised by a group of governing elites. It was never intended to be a system of Western-style *democratic self-government* that allows people to exercise their autonomous powers through universal suffrage (Fong, 2020).

Codification Under the 1983 Public Finance Ordinance

Fiscal conservatism and fiscal autonomy, the two pillars of British Hong Kong's budgetary institutions, were both products of decades-long historical processes. In the 1980s, Hong Kong's budgetary institutions entered into another important stage of development, when the institutional arrangements, originally administrative in nature but had been operational in the territory for decades, were formally codified into a local law by virtue of the 1983 *Public Finance Ordinance*.

After the granting of full fiscal autonomy by London in 1958, the original system of fiscal controls under the Colonial Regulations was no longer be applicable to Hong Kong and it was effectively replaced by the local oversight of the Legislative Council Finance Committee (Rabushka, 1976: 34; Tang, 1993). Fully comprised of appointed unofficial members of the Legislative Council until 1984, the Finance Committee and its two subcommittees, namely the Establishment Sub-Committee and Public Works Sub-Committee, were responsible for scrutinizing and approving the expenditure proposals prepared by the Hong Kong government (Rabushka, 1976: 46–47).

Such a local system of fiscal controls was later formally codified into the Public Finance Ordinance, which was passed by the Hong Kong's Legislative Council in 1983 to serve as a comprehensive statutory framework for managing public budgeting (Finance Branch, 1995: 5). In short, the Public Finance Ordinance codified the long-standing budgetary institutions, which had already been operational under the predominance of the Financial Secretaries for decades in Hong Kong. That included the obligation of the Financial Secretary to lay before the Legislative Council the annual estimates of revenue and expenditure in the form of an Appropriation Bill before the commencement of the next following financial year (Section 5), the power of the Financial Secretary to submit proposals to the Finance Committee's consideration any changes to the approved estimates of expenditure (Section 8), the authority of the Financial Secretary to approve changes to the approved estimates of expenditure under the delegation of the Finance Committee (Section 8), the general duties of the Financial Secretary to supervise, control, and direct all matters relating to the financial affairs of the government (Section 10), the mandate of the Financial Secretary to make and give administrative regulations, directions, and instructions for carrying out the provisions of the Ordinance (Section 11), the responsibility of departmental Controlling Officers to obey all administrative regulations, directions, and instructions made by the Financial Secretary (Section 13), the authority of the Financial Secretary to make investment of money, borrow money, and establish funds (Sections 26, 27, and 29), and so forth (Table 2.2).[3]

Overall, the 1983 Public Finance Ordinance codified the decades-long colonial budgetary institutions into a clear, comprehensive statutory

Table 2.2 Extracts of major provisions of the public finance ordinance

Section	*Extracts*
5(1)	"The Financial Secretary shall cause to be prepared in each financial year estimates of the revenue and expenditure of the Government for the next following financial year, and shall cause such estimates to be laid before the Legislative Council before or as soon as practicable after the commencement of the financial year to which they relate."
8(1)	"Subject to this section, no changes shall be made to the approved estimates of expenditure except with the approval of the Finance Committee upon a proposal of the Financial Secretary."
8(3)	"The Finance Committee may delegate to the Financial Secretary the power to approve changes subject to such conditions, exceptions and limitations as are specified in the delegation."
8(4)	"The Financial Secretary, where a delegation by the Finance Committee under subsection (3) so provides, and subject to such conditions, exceptions and limitations as are specified in the delegation, may further delegate his power to approve changes to any public officer."
10	"The Financial Secretary shall, subject to this Ordinance and any other enactment, have the management of the finances of the Government and the supervision, control and direction of all matters relating to the financial affairs of the Government."
11(1)	"Without prejudice to any other provision of this Ordinance, the Financial Secretary may make such administrative regulations and give such administrative directions and instructions not inconsistent with this Ordinance as may appear to him to be necessary or expedient for the better carrying out of the provisions and purposes of this Ordinance and for the safety, economy and advantage of public moneys and Government property."

(*continued*)

[3]The latest version of the Public Finance Ordinance can be found in the Hong Kong e-Legislation at https://www.elegislation.gov.hk/hk/cap2. For an account of the major provisions of the Public Finance Ordinance, see Finance Branch (1995: 5–18).

Table 2.2 (continued)

Section	*Extracts*
13	"Every controlling officer shall obey all regulations made and directions or instructions given by the Financial Secretary under section 11 and shall, if so required, account to the Financial Secretary for the performance of his duties as controlling officer."
26(1)	"Subject to the provisions of any enactment, the Financial Secretary in his discretion may authorize the investment of moneys forming part of the general revenue in such manner as he may determine."
27(2)	"Notwithstanding the provisions of any other enactment, the Financial Secretary may borrow by means of advances from any bank, by means of a fluctuating overdraft or otherwise, such sums as may be required to meet day to day payments and any interest or service charges in respect of such sums shall be charged on the general revenue."
29(1)	"The Legislative Council may by resolution provide for the establishment of funds to which moneys appropriated for the purpose, and such other moneys received for the purposes of the Government as may be specified in the resolution, may be credited and from which moneys may, under the authority of a funds warrant issued by the Financial Secretary, be expended for the purposes for which the funds were established subject to such conditions, exceptions and limitations as may be specified in the resolution."

framework. Therefore, some budgeting scholars had described the significance of the Public Finance Ordinance as the "single most important legislation governing the allocation of scare resources" in Hong Kong (Lo, 1990: 87).[4]

Constitutionalization Under the 1984 Sino-British Joint Declaration and the 1990 Basic Law

Hong Kong budgetary institutions had entered the most critical stage of development during the sovereignty transition period of the 1980s and 1990s, with its two major pillars of fiscal conservatism and fiscal autonomy

[4] By virtue of the 1983 Public Finance Ordinance, a comprehensive set of internal administrative regulations, directions, and instructions had been formulated and put into practice within the Hong Kong government in the 1980s and the 1990s to govern the day-to-day operation of the public budgeting activities. This set of administrative rules covers several types of government documents, with different scopes and purposes, namely the Financial and Accounting Regulations as well as the Financial Circulars, Memoranda, Guides issued by the Finance Branch. For an account of such administrative rules, see Lo, 1990: 88–91.

constitutionalized by virtue of the *1984 Sino-British Joint Declaration* and the *1990 HKSAR Basic Law*.

The 1984 Sino-British Joint Declaration was officially called the *Joint Declaration of the Government of the United Kingdom of Great Britain and Northern Ireland and the Government of the People's Republic of China on the Question of Hong Kong*. It was the product of two-year long negotiation between Britain and China over the political future of Hong Kong, through which the two countries finally agreed that Hong Kong would be transited from a British crown colony into a Chinese Special Administrative Region on 1 July 1997.[5]

The constitutional importance of the 1984 Sino-British Joint Declaration lies not only in confirming that Hong Kong's sovereignty would be handed over by Britain to China in 1997, but also in laying down the overall constitutional arrangements of post-1997 Hong Kong as a territorial autonomy, officially called the model of "One Country Two Systems" (OCTS). Because at that time the consensus of Britain and China was to maintain the "status quo" of Hong Kong for the broader purpose of promoting "smooth transition," most of the provisions of the 1984 Sino-British Joint Declaration were primarily designed to maintain the institutional continuity in Hong Kong before and after 1997. Consequently, Hong Kong's fiscal autonomy, together with all those de facto autonomous powers that had been operational since the 1950s, was de jure recognized by virtue of the Main Articles and Annex I of the 1984 Sino-British Joint Declaration as an international treaty (Ure, 2012: 1; Fong, 2020).[6]

Article 3(12) of the 1984 Sino-British Joint Declaration states that the Chinese National People's Congress (NPC) would enact a "Basic Law" to stipulate the territorial autonomous arrangements of the HKSAR. It is important to note that the Joint Declaration had only constitutionalized the fiscal autonomy of Hong Kong, but it did not contain any clause about fiscal conservatism, another major pillar of the colonial budgetary institutions. Fiscal conservatism was finally constitutionalized, together with

[5] Full text of the 1984 Sino-British Joint Declaration: https://www.cmab.gov.hk/en/issues/joint3.htm.

[6] Officially signed on 19 December 1984, the 1984 Sino-British Joint Declaration was registered under the United Nations by China on 12 June 1985 (Registration Number: 23391). See the online register of the Treaty Section of the Office of Legal Affairs of the United Nations at: https://treaties.un.org/Pages/showDetails.aspx?objid=08000002800d4d6e.

fiscal autonomy that was already enshrined in the Joint Declaration, during the drafting process of the Basic Law in 1985 to 1990.

Fiscal conservatism was, in fact, one of the major controversies during the drafting process of the Basic Law. Officially called the *Basic Law of the Hong Kong Special Administrative Region of the People's Republic of China*, the formal drafting process of the Basic Law was begun in April 1985 when the NPC set up the Basic Law Drafting Committee (BLDC) and the Basic Law Consultative Committee (BLCC)—the former was comprised of altogether 59 Mainland and Hong Kong members and was responsible for coordinating the drafting process, while the latter entirely consisted of 180 Hong Kong members appointed by Beijing from different sectors, responsible for canvassing community views regarding the drafts.[7] The BLDC was divided into five sub-groups, each of which focused on one main area of the Basic Law, namely "the Relationship Between the Central Authorities and the HKSAR," "the Fundamental Rights and Duties of Residents," "the Political Structure," "the Economy," and "the Education Science, Technology, Culture, Sports and Religion," with a "General Working Group" responsible for making the overall adjustment and revision of the drafts submitted by the sub-groups (Ghai, 1999: 58).

During the drafting process, the incorporation of the colonial fiscal conservatism into the Basic Law was the most contentious issue within the Economy Sub-Group (Tang, 1989). The crux of the debates within the Economy Sub-Group was whether and to what extent the major principles of the fiscal conservatism, in particular balanced budgets and low tax policy, should be constitutionalized into the Basic Law together with the notion of fiscal autonomy, which was already enshrined by the Sino-British Joint Declaration. Two opposing views emerged in the debates, the pro-fiscal conservatism camp argued that it was necessary to actualize the so-called constitutional economics[8] in the Basic Law mandating the future

[7]For an account of the Basic Law's drafting process, see Chan and Clark (1991).

[8]Constitutional economics is a popular economic school of thought championed by American economist James M. Buchanan in the 1980s. It argues that the only way to stop politicians from buying popular support through expanding government services is to impose a constitutional requirement of balanced budgets. The theories of constitutional economics were adopted by the business sector in Hong Kong to justify the need for constitutionalization of fiscal conservation during the drafting process of the Basic Law. See, Tang, 1989 and Ghai, 1999: 233–234.

Hong Kong government to practise balanced budgets and a low tax policy; while the anti-fiscal conservatism camp insisted that such policy guidelines should be simplified and replaced by a general provision of fiscal autonomy stipulating that "the HKSAR shall deal on its own with financial matters" (Tang, 1989: 2). Finally, the pro-fiscal conservatism camp prevailed in the drafting process and their views were essentially endorsed by the whole BLDC (Scott, 2010: 153), with the notion of fiscal autonomy constitutionalized into Article 106 of the Basic Law and conservative fiscal principles of balanced budgets and low tax policy incorporated as Articles 107 and 108, respectively, in the Basic Law finally promulgated by the NPC on 4 April 1990.[9]

The constitutionalization of fiscal conservatism was a triumph of the local business elites, the strong advocates of applying constitutional economics to the context of Hong Kong (Ghai, 1999: 233–234 and 238–239). During the drafting process, Wong Po-Yan, a local business tycoon and also the co-convener of the Basic Law Economy Sub-Group, insisted on many occasions the pressing need to constitutionalize the fiscal principles of balanced budgets and low tax policy, considering it as an essential mechanism to counter-balance the welfare demands of those "free lunch groups" under the future democratizing Legislative Council (Tang, 1989). Such an outcome was in fact part of the broader political process of the formation of a new China-centred government-business alliance during the transitional period of the 1980s to the 1990s, when the interests of the business sector was institutionalized by Beijing into the HKSAR establishment in exchange for their political support (Fong, 2014: 103–118).

Consequently, the major pillars of Hong Kong's budgetary institutions not only survived the sovereignty transition period of the 1980s–1990s, they had been entrenched under the post-1997 territorial arrangements by virtue of the 1984 Sino-British Joint Declaration and the 1990 HKSAR Basic Law (Table 2.3).

[9]Articles 106 and 107 had been debated and revised for several rounds, before they were passed and incorporated into the final version of the Basic Law. For an account of how different versions of Articles 106 and 107 were debated, see Tang, 1989.

Table 2.3 Constitutionalization of fiscal autonomy and fiscal conservatism under the 1984 Sino-British Joint Declaration and the 1990 HKSAR Basic Law

	1984 Sino-British Joint Declaration	*1990 HKSAR Basic Law*
Fiscal autonomy	Article 3(8): "The Hong Kong Special Administrative Region will have independent finances. The Central People's Government will not levy taxes on the Hong Kong Special Administrative Region." Annex I (Section V, Number 1): "The Hong Kong Special Administrative Region shall deal on its own with financial matters, including disposing of its financial resources and drawing up its budgets and its final accounts. The Hong Kong Special Administrative Region shall report its budgets and final accounts to the Central People's Government for the record." Annex I (Section V, Number 2): "The Central People's Government shall not levy taxes on the Hong Kong Special Administrative Region. The Hong Kong Special Administrative Region shall use its financial revenues exclusively for its own purposes and they shall not be handed over to the Central People's Government. The systems by which taxation and public expenditure must be approved by the legislature, and by which there is accountability to the legislature for all public expenditure, and the system for auditing public accounts shall be maintained."	Article 106: "The Hong Kong Special Administrative Region shall have independent finances. The Hong Kong Special Administrative Region shall use its financial revenues exclusively for its own purposes, and they shall not be handed over to the Central People's Government. The Central People's Government shall not levy taxes in the Hong Kong Special Administrative Region."

(*continued*)

Table 2.3 (continued)

	1984 Sino-British Joint Declaration	*1990 HKSAR Basic Law*
Fiscal conservation	–	Article 107: "The Hong Kong Special Administrative Region shall follow the principle of keeping the expenditure within the limits of revenues in drawing up its budget, and strive to achieve a fiscal balance, avoid deficits and keep the budget commensurate with the growth rate of its gross domestic product." Article 108: "The Hong Kong Special Administrative Region shall practise an independent taxation system. The Hong Kong Special Administrative Region shall, taking the low tax policy previously pursued in Hong Kong as reference, enact laws on its own concerning types of taxes, tax rates, tax reductions, allowances and exemptions, and other matters of taxation."

Conclusion

This chapter analyses the Hong Kong budgetary institutions as products of a three-stage historical process: the formation stage tracing back to the founding of the Hong Kong colony in 1841; the codification stage under the 1983 Public Finance Ordinance; the constitutionalization stage under the 1984 Sino-British Joint Declaration and the 1990 HKSAR Basic Law.

Through a historical perspective, this chapter demonstrates why and how the major pillars of the colonial budgetary institutions, namely the fiscal conservatism and the fiscal autonomy, have become so immutable in Hong Kong that government officials instinctively stick to them throughout the pre-1997 British rule and the post-1997 Chinese rule. Such a high degree of institutional continuity was not accidental, but the consequence of the interaction of the historical forces of the British Empire and the local government-business alliance.

Further Readings

- Rabushka, A. (1976). *Value for money: The Hong Kong budgetary process.* Stanford, CA: Hoover Institution Press.

The only book-length study of the formation and operation of Hong Kong budgetary institutions under the British Empire.

- Tang, S. H. (1989). *Fiscal constitution and the Basic Law (Draft) of Hong Kong* (BRC working papers series; ES 89005). Hong Kong: Business Research Centre, Hong Kong Baptist College.

A good account of the debates over fiscal conservatism in Hong Kong during the drafting process of the Basic Law.

- Goodstadt, L. F. (2010). Fiscal Freedom and the Making of Hong Kong's Capitalist Society. *China Information, 24*(3), 273–294.

A clear, archive-based account of the formation of Hong Kong's fiscal autonomy under the British rule.

Bibliography

Blöchliger, H. (2005). *Fiscal Autonomy of Sub-Central Governments.* OECD Network on Fiscal Relations Across Governments Working Papers, No. 2. Paris: OECD.

Branch, F. (1995). *Practitioner's Guide: Management of Public Finances.* Government Printer.

Brendon, P. (2007). *The Decline and Fall of the British Empire 1781–1997.* Jonathan Cape Bright.

Chan, M. K., & Clark, D. J. (1991). Democracy Derailed: Realpolitik in the Making of the Hong Kong Basic Law, 1985–90. In M. K. Chan & D. J. Clark (Eds.), *The Hong Kong Basic Law: Blueprint for "Stability and Prosperity" Under Chinese Sovereignty?* (pp. 3–35). Hong Kong University Press.

Colonial Office. (1843). *Rules and Regulations for Her Majesty's Colonial Service.* Printed by George E. Eyre and William Spottiswoode, Printers to the Queen's Most Excellent Majesty, for Her Majesty's Stationery Office.

Drummond, P., & Mansoor, A. (2002). *Macroeconomic Management and the Devolution of Fiscal Powers.* IMF Working Paper 02/76, International Monetary Fund, Washington.

Fong, B. C. H. (2014). *Hong Kong's Governance Under Chinese Sovereignty: The Failure of the State-Business Alliance After 1997*. Routledge.

Fong, B. C. H. (2015). The Politics of Budget Surpluses: The Case of China's HKSAR. *International Review of Administrative Sciences, 81*(1), 134–157.

Fong, B. C. H. (2020). Practicing Autonomy Within a Communist State: Hong Kong's Autonomy from Handover to Anti-Extradition Bill Movement, 1997 to 2019. *Communist and Post-Communist Studies, 53*(4), 68–90.

Gardner, L., & Roy, T. (2020). *The Economic History of Colonialism*. Bristol University Press.

Ghai, Y. (1999). *Hong Kong's New Constitutional Order: The Resumption of Chinese Sovereignty and the Basic Law*. Hong Kong University Press.

Goodstadt, L. F. (2009). *Uneasy Partners: The Conflict Between Public Interest and Private Profit Interest in Hong Kong*. Hong Kong University Press.

Goodstadt, L. F. (2010). Fiscal Freedom and the Making of Hong Kong's Capitalist Society. *China Information, 24*(3), 273–294.

Hallerberg, M., Rolf, S., & Von Hagen, J. (2009). The Political Economy of Budget Deficits. In A. Ayuso-I-Casals, S. Deroose, E. Flores, & L. Moulin (Eds.), *Policy Instruments for Sound Fiscal Policies Fiscal Rules and Institutions* (pp. 127–148). Palgrave Macmillan.

Hooghe, L., Marks, G., & Schakel, A. H. (2016). *Measuring Regional Authority*. Oxford University Press.

Imbeau, L., & Pétry, F. (2004). The Political Economy of Public Deficits. In L. Imbeau & F. Pétry (Eds.), *Politics, Institutions, and Fiscal Policy: Deficits and Surpluses in Federated States* (pp. 1–19). Lexington Books.

Jansen, J. C., Osterhammel, J., & Riemer, J. (2017). *Decolonization: A Short History*. Princeton University Press.

Levine, P. (2013). *The British Empire Sunrise to Sunset* (2nd ed.). Pearson Education.

Lo, C. S. S. (1990). *Public Budgeting in Hong Kong: An Incremental Decision-Making Approach*. Writers' and Publishers' Cooperative.

Marquand, D. (2008). *Britain Since 1918: The Strange Career of British Democracy*. Weidenfeld & Nicolson.

Miners, N. (1998). *The Government and Politics of Hong Kong* (5th ed.). Oxford University Press.

Pola, G. (2016). *Principles and Practices of Fiscal Autonomy: Experiences, Debates and Prospects*. Routledge.

Rabushka, A. (1976). *Value for Money: The Hong Kong Budgetary Process*. Hoover Institution Press.

Rabushka, A. (1979). *Hong Kong: A Study in Economic Freedom*. University of Chicago Press.

Raudla, R. (2014). Budgetary Institutions. In J. Backhaus (Ed.), *Encyclopedia of Law and Economics* (pp. 1–9). Springer.

Schmitt, D. A. (2006). *The Bechuanaland Pioneers and Gunners*. Praeger.
Scott, I. (1989). *Political Change and the Crisis of Legitimacy in Hong Kong*. Oxford University Press.
Scott, I. (2010). *The Public Sector in Hong Kong*. Hong Kong University Press.
Share, C. (2007). *Where Empires Collided: Russian and Soviet Relations with Hong Kong, Taiwan, and Macao*. The Chinese University of Hong Kong Press.
Tang, S. H. (1989). *Fiscal Constitution and the Basic Law (Draft) of Hong Kong (BRC Working Papers Series; ES 89005)*. Business Research Centre, Hong Kong Baptist College.
Tang, S. H. (1993). *Fiscal Legislation and Financial Control in Hong Kong (BRC Working Papers Series; ES 92031)*. Business Research Centre, Hong Kong Baptist College.
Ure, G. (2012). *Governors, Politics, and the Colonial Office: Public Policy in Hong Kong, 1918–58*. Hong Kong University Press.
Von Hagen, J. (2007). Budgeting Institutions for better Fiscal Performance. In A. Shah (Ed.), *Budgeting and Budgetary Institutions* (pp. 27–51). World Bank.

CHAPTER 3

Budgetary Decision-Making

Budgetary decision-making is "a political process in harmonizing varied/ conflicting interests among constituents" (Yamamoto, 2018: 476). Because government resources are always limited and taxation is never popular, continuous balancing of different actors' competing expenditure requests and revenue proposals is central to the budgetary decision-making of all governments. Consequently, while budgetary decision-making is being structured by the basic scene set by budgetary institutions, it is fundamentally a process replete with politics and the final outcome is determined by the political interaction of the actors involved, spanning from executive, legislature, and judiciary to organized interest groups, the media, and the public (Lee et al., 2013: 16; Rubin, 2020: 305; Khan, 2019: 178–179).

This chapter traces the transformation of the budgetary decision-making in Hong Kong, using the transitional period of the 1980–1990s as the dividing line. In Chap. 2, I have already demonstrated why and how the budgetary institutions have remained unchanged, or even entrenched,

Originally published in a slightly different form under the title of "The Politics of Budget Surpluses: The Case of China's HKSAR," reprinted from *International Review of Administrative Sciences*, 2015; 81(1), 134–157, by permission of SAGE Publications.

B. C. H. Fong, *Hong Kong Public Budgeting*, Hong Kong Studies Reader Series, https://doi.org/10.1007/978-981-16-5363-6_3

during the transitional period of the 1980–1990s—the formal, statutory institutions for managing public budgeting in Hong Kong was codified under the 1983 Public Finance Ordinance and the systems of fiscal autonomy and fiscal conservatism were constitutionalized by the 1984 Sino-British Joint Declaration and the 1990 Hong Kong Special Administrative Region (HKSAR) Basic Law. Yet, the entrenchment of the budgetary institutions in the 1980–1990s did not mean that the budgetary decision-making remained intact. Instead, owing to the internal and external driving forces both within and outside the Hong Kong government since the 1980–1990s, a new interaction pattern of budgetary actors has emerged and significantly transformed the budgetary decision-making from the previous *bureaucratic bargaining model* into the new *pluralistic bargaining model.*

Bureaucratic Bargaining Model Before the 1980–1990s

Because budgetary decision-making is a political process, it must be discussed in the broader context of changing political systems, forces, and events. In this connection, the predominant feature of British Hong Kong's political system was the concentration of powers in the hands of bureaucrats and such a power structure had undoubtedly shaped the budgetary decision-making.

In accordance with the Letters Patent and the Royal Instructions, the two constitutional documents issued by London in respect of Hong Kong, the British Governor was at the centre of the colonial power structure who "personified the combination of executive and legislative, and civil and military powers"—the Governor was the head of government, chairman of the Legislative Council, and the commander-in-chief of British military forces in Hong Kong; he also had the power to appoint all members of the Legislative Council (Cheung, 2007). While constitutionally speaking, the colonial Governors had almost autocratic powers; they came and went on a regular basis and could only govern with the co-operation and support of the permanent civil service (Miners, 1998: 70; Cheung, 2007). On the other hand, although the Legislative Council had the constitutional powers to approve the government's budgets and supplementary provisions particularly after the granting of fiscal autonomy in 1958, it was wholly constituted by legislators appointed by the Governor up to 1985. Senior civil servants were appointed as official members to form a majority in the legislature, while unofficial members, mainly business and professional sectors also owned their allegiance to the colonial government. Such an appointment system enabled the bureaucrats to dominate the legislative process and the role of the Legislative Council was confined to rubber-stamp the government's budgetary proposals (Lo, 1990: 57). In view of the above, the bureaucrats governed in the absence of accountable politics (Cheung, 1998) and British Hong Kong was often described by scholars as a "bureaucratic polity" (Lau, 1982) or an "administrative state" (Harris, 1988).

Within this bureaucrat-dominated political system, the Financial Secretary and the Finance Branch under his leadership exercised strongest influences over the budgetary decision-making. In British Hong Kong, although the Financial Secretary only ranked third in the colonial hierarchy after the Governor and the Colonial Secretary (re-titled as Chief Secretary in 1976), he was virtually an autonomous dictator over budgetary decision-making—a "master of the budgetary process" (Rabushka, 1976: 56). The superior status of the Financial Secretary was reflected in a political hearsay that John Cowperthwaite, the Financial Secretary of the 1960s, refused to be promoted to the Colonial Secretary because the position of Financial Secretary played a better defined and more independent role than the Colonial Secretary (Cheung, 2006). The Finance Branch, located in the fifth floor of the Government Secretariat and headed by the Secretary for the Treasury under the purview of the Financial Secretary, was also internally referred by government officials as an "all-powerful policy branch" and had been the first among equals vis-à-vis all other policy branches (Rabushka, 1979: 39; Cheung, 2006).

Why were the Financial Secretary and the Finance Branch so powerful? The superior status of the Financial Secretary over the budgetary decision-making was built upon several factors. First, the Financial Secretary built and exercised his strong influence by virtue of his strategic, constitutional role as a "protector of the public purse" of the Hong Kong colony (Lo, 1990: 68). As the principal official held responsible for fulfilling the fiscal requirements imposed by the Colonial Office under the Colonial Regulations, the Financial Secretary was much more than a treasury official handling the preparation of the annual budgets, but he was a key policy-maker "heavily involved in wide-ranging activities which bear upon the fiscal health of government and the economic health of the colony. Any government policy with fiscal or economic implications must involve the Financial Secretary" (Rabushka, 1976: 56). By virtue of his strategic powers to approve expenditure items and to examine the financial implications of all policy proposals, the influences of the Financial Secretary (and his treasury officials from the Finance Branch) went beyond the ambit of budget allocation and spilled over into the broader governance functions of policy formulation and implementation. It was under such a context that the Financial Secretary had become as a principal policy-maker in the Government Secretariat and the Finance Branch had evolved into an "all-powerful policy branch" running the British Hong Kong government by default—because they advised all policy branches and departments on the financial feasibility and implications of proposed policies; they coordinated the preparation of all papers to the Finance Committee of the Legislative Council for securing funding for new policies; they oversaw all policy branches and departments in their preparation of annual estimates of expenditure planned for their existing policies (Rabushka, 1979: 40–41).[1]

Second, the Financial Secretary maintained his political autonomy from the Governor and the Colonial Secretary. Under the colonial power structure, while all powers were constitutionally vested with the Governor, he always delegated much of his budgetary powers to the Financial Secretary (Rabushka, 1979: 65; Cheung, 2006). Even the Executive Council under the chairmanship of the Governor seldom discussed public budgeting and other financial issues, and the Executive Councillors were often briefed on the details of the annual Appropriation Bills a few days before its introduction into the Legislative Council (Tang, 1993). The Colonial Secretary, who was constitutionally one rank above the Financial Secretary and was the civil service head responsible for the general administration of the Government Secretariat, also exercised limited influence over budgetary decision-making. The reason was that the Colonial Secretary had no power to overrule the Financial Secretary, who reported directly to the Governor over his areas of responsibilities on public budgeting and economic matters (Rabushka, 1976: 54–55).

Third, the Financial Secretary was largely insulated from the pressure of external oversight institution, namely the Legislative Council. Because the

[1] Lo (1990: 68) observed that the Financial Secretary held strategic advantage in the internal policy deliberation process, because he was the only person who had the comprehensive information of the totally available resources. Therefore, the Financial Secretary was in the all-powerful position in endorsing or rejecting a policy proposal on public budgeting grounds.

Legislative Council was wholly appointed by the Governor until 1984, election competition, party bargaining, and interest group politics were almost absent in the pre-1990s Hong Kong. So long as the budgetary proposals formulated by the government were consistent with the government-business alliance's consensus of fiscal conservatism (Fong, 2014: 89), the bureaucrats faced little opposition from the appointed unofficial members. Consequently, budgetary decision-making for much of the British colonial time was essentially closed and well insulated from external legislative pressures, enabling the bureaucrats, particularly the Financial Secretary to control the overall resources allocation (Scott, 2010: 149–150).

In view of the above, the budgetary decision-making in British Hong Kong, going right up to the 1980s, was largely confined to the interaction between two sets of players within the colonial bureaucracy, that is the Central Budget Agency (i.e. the Financial Secretary and his treasury officials from the Finance Branch) and the Budget Spenders (i.e. government officials from different policy branches and departments) (Rabushka, 1976: 128; Cheung, 2005). In this connection, the budgetary decision-making in British Hong Kong was characterized by bureaucratic competition for financial resources: with the Central Budget Agency adhering to its constitutional position of maintaining centralized financial control and of constraining government expenditure through rigorous scrutiny of policy proposals, while the Budget Spenders sought a maximum degree of delegated authority and attempting to expand their budgets. Such a bureaucratic bargaining model of budgetary decision-making was featured with continuous internal bargaining and negotiations within the colonial bureaucracy (Lo, 1990; Cheung, 2005) (Fig. 3.1).

Pluralistic Bargaining Model Since the 1980–1990s

There were both internal and external driving forces within and outside the Hong Kong government since the 1980–1990s. The coupling of such forces had finally resulted in a corresponding shift in the model of the budgetary decision-making.

The internal driving force was arising from a number of reforms and changes within the Hong Kong government which, by intention or default, undermined the Financial Secretary's long-standing dominant position in the budgetary decision-making. Several changes were particularly relevant here. Firstly, the Star Chamber, which is co-chaired by the

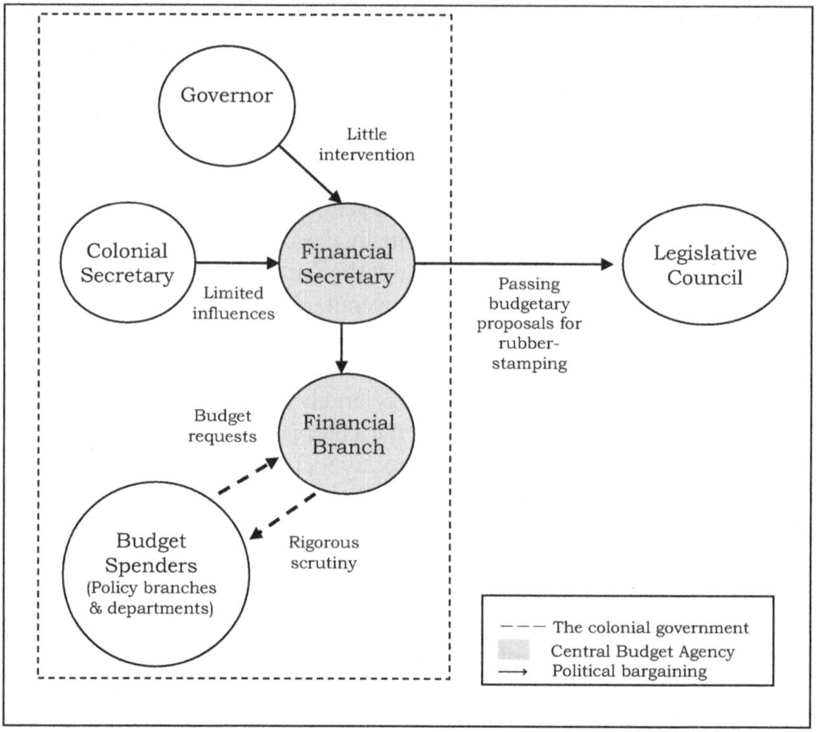

Fig. 3.1 Bureaucratic bargaining model of budgetary decision-making

Chief Secretary and the Financial Secretary and is comprised of the Secretary for the Treasury and the Secretary for the Civil Service, was set up in 1994 as a mechanism to decide the allocation of resources for financing new policies in the annual Resources Allocation Exercise (RAE). Under this arrangement, the Chief Secretary was for the first time given a formal, important role to play in the budget allocation and the Financial Secretary's superior status in the budgetary decision-making has somewhat been weakened (Cheung, 2005).

Secondly, one of the major themes of public sector reforms in Hong Kong since the 1990s was the devolution of financial powers. Financial reforms including the setting up of resource management units in policy branches in 1994 and the introduction of the operating expenditure envelope and one-line vote in 2003–2004 have both significantly enhanced the financial autonomy of Policy Secretaries—who have become political executives instead of career civil servants since the implementation of the Principal Officials Accountability System (POAS) in 2002 (Cheung, 2006). Throughout this reform process, the originally all-powerful Finance Branch, once renamed Finance Bureau in 1997, had even lost its independent bureau status and was integrated into the new Financial Services and the Treasury Bureau (FSTB) in the name of the Treasury Branch under the POAS introduced in 2002 (Cheung, 2005).

Thirdly, unlike the colonial Governor who usually adopted a hands-off approach on budgetary matters, the HKSAR Chief Executive now assumes a more presidential style of leadership. As a result, under the post-1997 Chinese rule the Financial Secretary's annual Budget Speeches have been increasingly integrated into the Chief Executive's Policy Addresses, which often preset spending priorities (Cheung, 2006). All in all, the Financial Secretary is no more a "master of the budgetary process" as in the British colonial past and there have been an increasing form of power-sharing between the Central Budget Agency (i.e. Financial Secretary and the Treasury Branch) and Budget Spenders (i.e. Policy Secretaries of different policy bureaux),[2] with the former now concentrated on macro-budget allocations while the latter focused on meso-budget allocations to departments within their purview.

The external driving force was principally the partial democratization of the Legislative Council. The introduction of functional constituencies in 1985 and directly elected seats in 1991 had effectively turned the Legislative Council from the rubber stamp of the executive in colonial time into an independent opposition chamber in the 1990s (Cheung, 2007). After the handover, the number of directly elected seats had been gradually further expanded, transforming the Legislative Council a partially democratized legislature (Table 3.1). Returned either by direct elections or by functional constituencies, both pro-democracy and pro-regime legislators have organized themselves into political parties (Table 3.2).

The rise of party politics implied that the bureaucrats could no longer dominate the budgetary decision-making as in the past. By exercising their financial control power including the votes on the annual budgets and the powers to approve government's supplementary provisions, legislators can now force the government to make policy concessions to cater for the interests of their own electoral constituents. Such a new modus operandi

[2] Policy branches were re-named policy bureaux after 1997.

Table 3.1 Partial-democratization of legislative council

Year	*Appointed*		*Elected*			*Total*
	Official	*Unofficial*	*Election Committee*	*Functional constituency*	*Directly elected*	
1985–1988	11	22	12	12	0	57
1988–1991	11	22	12	14	0	59
1991–1995	3	17	0	21	18	59
1995–1997	0	0	10	30	20	60
1997–1998	0	0	60[a]	0	0	60[a]
1998–2000	0	0	10	30	20	60
2000–2004	0	0	6	30	24	60
2004–2008	0	0	0	30	30	60
2008–2012	0	0	0	30	30	60
2012–2016	0	0	0	35	35	70
2012–2016	0	0	0	35	35	70

Source: Adapted from Ma, 2007 (for data before 1997); adapted from official data drawn from the Electoral Affairs Commission's website at https://www.eac.gov.hk (for data after 1997)

[a]The Chinese government disbanded the Legislative Council formed in 1995 and replaced it with the Provisional Legislative Council composed of 60 members all returned by the Election Committee

Table 3.2 Partisan distribution in the Legislative Council (2000–2016)

	2000	*2004*	*2008*	*2012*	*2016*
Pro-democracy camp	20 (33.3%)	25 (41.7%)	23 (38.3%)	27 (38.6%)	30 (42.9%)
Pro-regime camp	40 (66.7%)	35 (58.3%)	37 (61.7%)	43 (61.4%)	40 (57.1%)
Total	60 (100%)	60 (100%)	60 (100%)	70 (100%)	70 (100%)

Source: Adapted from Ma (2020)

of electoral and party politics has unavoidably resulted in more and more bargaining between government officials and political parties over the budget allocations (Cheung, 2005; Ma, 2007: 111). Worse still for the Hong Kong government after 1997, the Chief Executive was legally prohibited to be a member of political party under the Chief Executive Election Ordinance (Cap 569)[3] and therefore the government has so far

[3]Section 31(1) the Chief Executive Election Ordinance stated that "A person declared under section 28 as elected at an election shall, within 7 working days after the declaration—(a) publicly make a statutory declaration to the effect that he is not a member of any political party; and (b) lodge with the Returning Officer a written undertaking to the effect that he

remained a non-partisan administration, despite the fact that the partial-democratization of the Legislative Council has resulted in the rise of political parties in the legislative arena. As a consequence of the disconnection between the executive and the legislature, apart from facing the challenges of pro-democracy parties, the pro-regime parties are not stable coalition partners of the Hong Kong government and the Chief Executive is facing growing difficulties in engineering a stable support base in the Legislative Council (Fong, 2018). Thus, while constitutional issues under the OCTS model remain the major dividing line between political parties in Hong Kong, the differences among parties on non-constitutional issues including public budgeting are less apparent. On many occasions, legislators across the political spectrum often join hands to exert pressure on the Hong Kong government (Ma, 2012).

As a consequence of the above internal and external driving forces, budgetary decision-making after the 1980s–1990s is not a mere bureaucratic game anymore, but it has been increasingly driven by political dynamics within the legislative and civil society arenas (Cheung, 2005, 2006). Nowadays, the budgetary decision-making has been evolved into a competition for financial resources by various political actors—the Financial Secretary needs to bargain intensively with political parties and interest groups over the formulation of budgetary proposals on the one hand, while political executives and bureaucrats of various policy bureaux also concurrently engage in continuous consultations with different stakeholders over the resource allocation at their own bureau level on the other hand (Scott, 2010: 173) (Fig. 3.2).

The Cases of 1991 and 1992 Budgets

The political controversies surrounding both the 1991–1992 and 1992–1993 budgets were landmark incidents that symbolized the shift of budgetary decision-making from a bureaucratic bargaining model to a pluralistic bargaining model.

On 6 March 1991, the Financial Secretary Piers Jacobs announced the 1991–1992 budget, proposing to increase 200% of tobacco tax and to

will not, if appointed as the Chief Executive—(i) become a member of any political party; or (ii) do any act that has the effect of subjecting himself to the discipline of any political party, during his term of office as the Chief Executive." Full text of the Ordinance is available at: https://www.elegislation.gov.hk/hk/cap569.

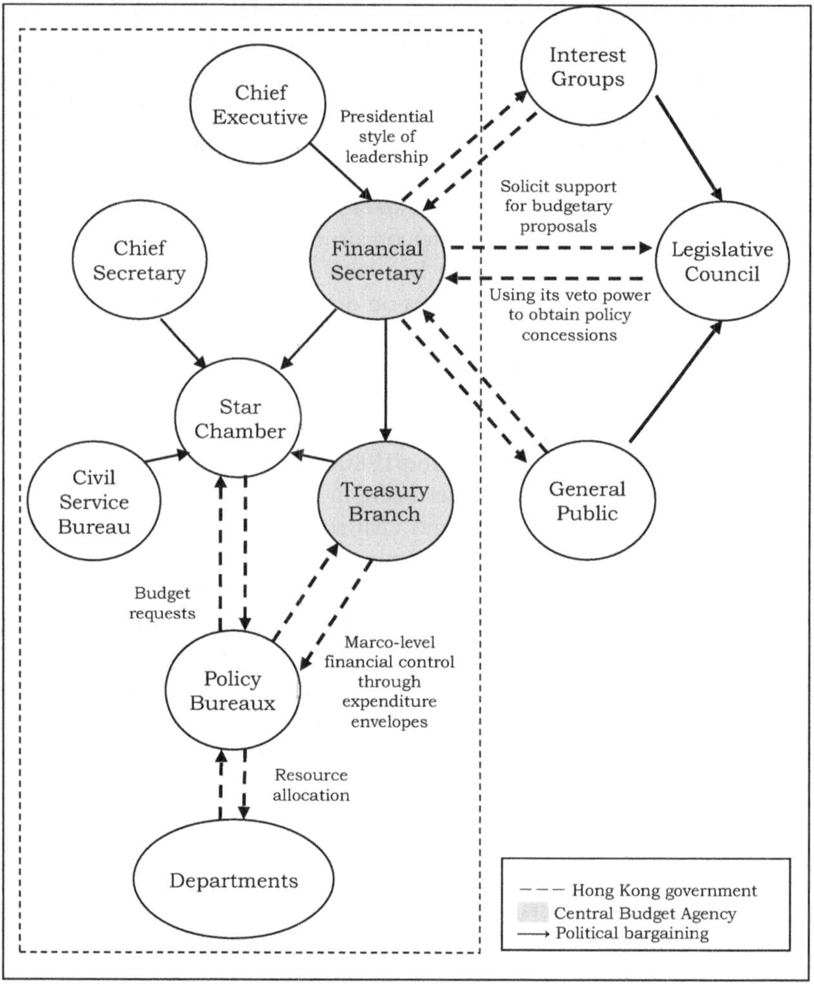

Fig. 3.2 The pluralistic bargaining model of budgetary decision-making

raise other government fees such as vehicle ownership transfer fee and light van registration fee. The proposals met with fierce opposition across the Legislative Council as well as strong public backlash. To pacify the opposition, especially those legislators who threatened to veto the budget, the Financial Secretary finally backed down on his plans and reduced the increase in tobacco tax from 200% to 100%. It was for the first time in Hong Kong history that the budget was amended after the announcement in the Budget Speech.[4]

A similar drama happened again in the 1992–1993 budget. In March 1992, the new Financial Secretary Hamish Macleod delivered his maiden Budget Speech proposing to increase the general rates from 5.5% to 6.0%. Once again, the proposal had attracted objections from a majority of Legislative Councillors and the public. Fearing that the amendment bill to the Rates Ordinance would be defeated in the Legislative Council, the Financial Secretary backed down on his plan and withdrew the whole bill before voting.[5]

The embarrassing U-turns by Piers Jacobs and Hamish Macleod in the 1991–1992 and 1992–1993 budgets fully demonstrated that they were no longer "masters of the budgetary process" like their predecessors. After the 1991 and 1992 incidents, Hamish Macleod decided to institutionalize the pre-Budget Speech consultation exercises with the Legislative Council and the general public, the practices of which have been followed by his successors (Ma, 2007: 108–109)—Hamish Macleod even coined the term "Consensus Capitalism," using it to describe his new practice of securing legislative and public support through better balancing of fiscal conservatism and social equity (Chiu & Wong, 2005). This formally marked the replacement of the old bureaucratic bargaining model by a new pluralistic bargaining model in Hong Kong's budgetary decision-making.

The Case of 2003–2004 Budget

The pluralistic bargaining model, which involves a wide range of actors spanning from Chief Executive, Financial Secretary, and different Policy Secretaries to Legislative Councillors from different parties, interest groups, the media, and the public, has become a norm for budgetary decision-making after 1997. In this connection, the case of 2003–2004

[4] For an account of the incident, see Sung and Lee (1991: xii–xiv).

[5] For an account of the incident, see Tang (1993).

budget was an example in point to illustrate how pluralistic the post-1997 budgetary decision-making had become in times of budget deficits.

The centre of the controversy in the 2003–2004 budget was how best should the massive budget deficit be balanced, with a focus on whether, how, and to what extent should civil service pay be reduced. In the aftermath of the 1998 Asian Financial Crisis, Hong Kong encountered an unprecedented economic recession and a dramatic slump in property and stock markets, bringing about consecutive years of budget deficits for the Hong Kong government (Wong, 2009). In December 2002, the Chief Executive Tung Chee-hwa announced a deficit reduction framework. Setting an overall objective of restoring fiscal balance by 2006–2007, the Tung administration claimed to adopt a three-pronged approach of reviving the economy, strictly controlling expenditure and raising revenue appropriately. On controlling public expenditure, the Tung administration set a specific target, though with little implementation detail, to drastically reduce the operating expenditure to the level of $200 billion by 2006–2007 (which represented a sharp reduction of the whole Government Estimates by $20 billion) (Hong Kong Special Administrative Region Government, 2002).

The ballooning of the budget deficits resulted in growing pressures from international financial institutions, investment community, and local business sector, which expressed rising concerns over the implications of ballooning budget deficits on stability of Hong Kong's financial and monetary systems. For example, Eswar Prasad, Assistant to the Director of the International Monetary Fund (IMF)'s Asia and Pacific Department, openly called for the Hong Kong government to formulate a clear deficit reduction plan to bolster market confidence: "The IMF welcomes the government's objective of achieving a balanced budget by fiscal year 2006–2007. However, a well-specified deficit reduction plan will be essential to bolster market confidence in Hong Kong's macroeconomic policies. The government, however, should implement sizeable structural deficit reduction measures in the fiscal year 2003–2004. There should also be a commitment to more structural consolidation supported by concrete measures in next three years" (Dawn, 2003).

Because personal expenses accounted for more than 70% of government operating expenditure, business chambers and pro-business parties actively advocated that a drastic civil service pay reduction was essential to achieve the $20 billion savings target; while the major civil service unions fiercely resisted such a proposal, and the two mainstream parties of

Democratic Party and Democratic Alliance for the Betterment of Hong Kong also expressed reservation owing to their connections with union interests (Fong, 2008). Consequently, the Chief Executive Tung Chee-hwa and the Financial Secretary Anthony Leung were divided over the pace and scale of the reduction.[6]

Finally, the Hong Kong government resorted to a negotiation approach and reached a consensus with the major civil service unions on the pace and scale of the pay reduction—the adoption of the "zero-three-three" civil service pay reduction settlement in the 2003–2004 budget, through which the Hong Kong government and the major civil service unions agreed to freeze civil service pay in 2003 and to reduce by 3% from 1 January 2004 and another 3% from 1 January 2005 (Hong Kong Special Administrative Region Government, 2003). The intensive negotiation among different government officials, political parties, civil service unions, business chambers, and so forth, in the formulation of the 2003–2004 budget was a living example of the pluralistic bargaining model.

The Case of 2011–2012 Budget

If the 2003–2004 budget was a textbook example of deficit politics in Hong Kong, then the case of 2011–2012 budget provided a good illustration on how surplus politics had been played out under the post-1997 pluralistic bargaining model.

After struggling through the deficit politics in the early 2000s, the Hong Kong government had experienced budget surpluses for nine consecutive years after 2004–2005, thanks to the strong economic rebound and investment market recovery. In 2007–2008, the Hong Kong government achieved a record surplus of HKD123,650 million. Although in 2008–2009 the amount of surplus had dropped to HKD1450 million due to the economic slowdown triggered by global financial tsunami, the Hong Kong government reaped successive years of huge surpluses again starting from 2009–2010. On average, the Hong Kong government has sustained a budget surplus of HKD50,952 million from 2004–2005 to 2012–2013 (Fig. 3.3).

[6] Research showed that the Hong Kong government was divided into two camps over the civil service pay reduction. Chief Executive Tung Chee-hwa and the Secretary for the Civil Service Joseph Wong tended to pacify the civil service unions by adopting a moderate cut; while the Financial Secretary Anthony Leung insisted to restore civil service pay to the 1997 level by implementing a drastic one-off 6% reduction. For an analysis of the competing interests and agendas of different budgetary actors in the 2003–2004 budget, see Fong, 2008.

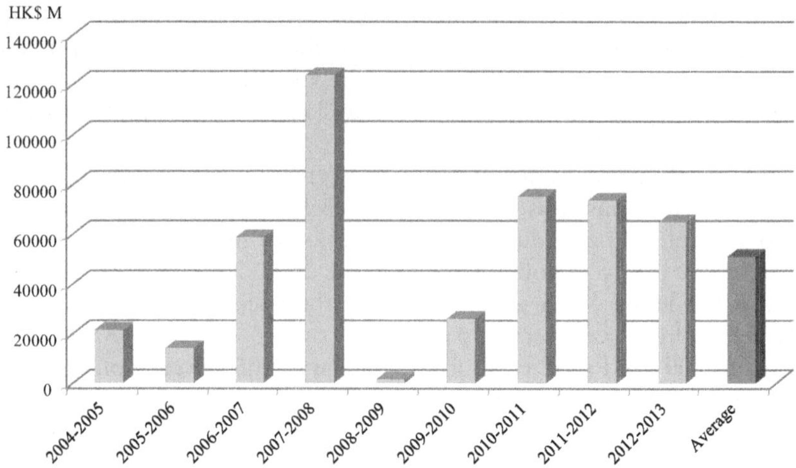

Fig. 3.3 Budget surpluses of Hong Kong government (from 2004–2005 to 2012–2013). (Source: Adapted from the statistical tables available at the Census and Statistics Department's website at http://www.censtatd.gov.hk)

In the face of consecutive years of surpluses, the Hong Kong government must decide on how best to allocate the budget surpluses, something that is unusual to most of the developed economies worldwide. For this purpose, the budgetary strategy adopted by John Tsang, the Financial Secretary since 2007 and a former civil servant, was twofold.

The first part of the budgetary strategy adopted by John Tsang was to spend billions of the budget surpluses on "one-off relief measures," while continuing to strictly control the growth of recurrent expenditure. Those one-off relief measures, nicknamed "one-off sweeties," normally included granting salaries tax rebates, waiving rates, paying extra allowance to recipients of Comprehensive Social Security Assistance and Old Age Allowance, waiving rental for public housing tenants, providing electricity subsidy, and so on. For a total of six budgets from 2008–2009 to 2013–2014, the total amount of "one-off sweeties" handed out by Tsang exceeded HKD198,803 million, meaning an average of HKD33,314 million spent on per year (Fig. 3.4). A closer examination on expenditure pattern of the Hong Kong government further indicated that in five- and ten-year time spans, it had increased its total expenditure by 60.7% and 57.8%

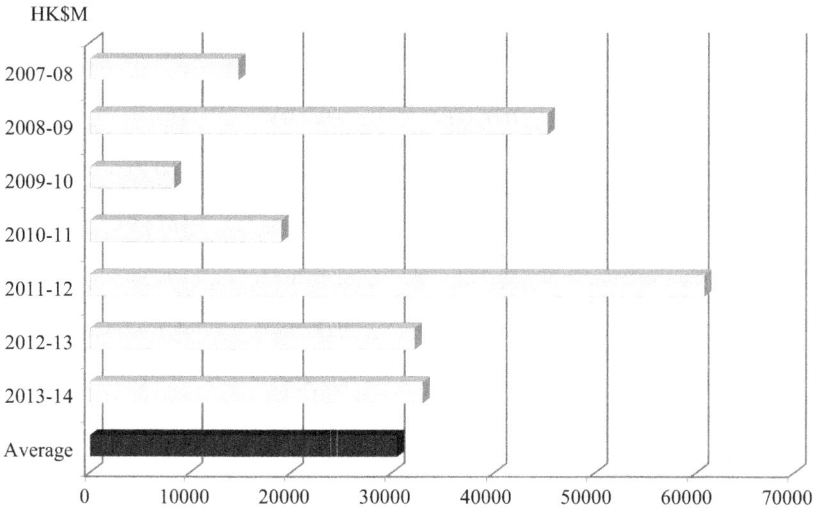

Fig. 3.4 One-off relief measures announced in Budget Speeches (from 2008–2009 to 2013–2014). (Source: Author's own research based on the annual Budget Speeches available at the website of the Hong Kong government's Budget at http://www.budget.gov.hk)

respectively, but the growth for recurrent expenses lagged behind the overall growth rate of total government expenditure and only experienced a relatively slow increase of 31.5% and 32.5% respectively; On the contrary, the growth rate for non-recurrent expenditure had increased sharply by 634.9% and 1352.4% respectively, indicating John Tsang's attempt to address public demands through non-recurrent one-off relief measures (Table 3.3). John Tsang had once publicly explained his preference of spending the budget surplus on "one-off relief measures" over expanding recurrent expenditure as follows:

> We adhere to the principles of prudent management of public finances, keeping expenditure within the limits of revenues and striving for a fiscal balance. This is not only due to the need to meet fully the requirements of the Basic Law, but is also based on the actual circumstances of Hong Kong as a small and open economy. As government revenue is highly susceptible to fluctuations and the flexibility in expenditure is low, it is necessary for us to maintain healthy and adequate fiscal reserves to cope with the impact

Table 3.3 Expenditure pattern of Hong Kong government (from 2007–2008 to 2012–2013)

Five-year time span	*2007–2008 (HK$M)*	*2012–2013 (HK$M)*	*Percentage change (%)*
Total revenue	358,465	442,150	+23.3%
Total expenditure	234,815	377,324	+60.7%
Total recurrent expenditure	199,446	262,321	+31.5%
Total non-recurrent expenditure	5021	36,897	+634.9%
Total capital expenditure	35,377	68,013	+92.3%
Ten-year time span	*2002–2003 (HK$M)*	*2012–2013 (HK$M)*	*Percentage change (%)*
Total revenue	177,489	442,150	+149.1%
Total expenditure	239,177	377,324	+57.8%
Total recurrent expenditure	198,004	262,321	+32.5%
Total non-recurrent expenditure	2540	36,897	+1352.4%
Total capital expenditure	41,740	68,013	+62.9%

Source: Author's own research based on the statistical tables available at the Census and Statistics Department's website at http://www.censtatd.gov.hk

Note: Because "non-recurrent expenditure" and "capital expenditure" usually fluctuate greatly every year, for a more accurate comparison the above table calculated these two items on a three-year average basis. As such, the sum of "recurrent expenditure," "non-recurrent expenditure," and "capital expenditure" is not equal to the "total government expenditure."

> economic cycles have on people's livelihood. Moreover, we must stay alert to the challenges ahead and be prepared for unexpected crises. In no case should we make, on account of an occasional increase in revenue, commitments that are difficult to sustain. This will bring nothing but tax increases and reduced competitiveness for future generations. (Hong Kong Special Administrative Region Government, 2011)

The second part of John Tsang's budgetary strategy was to set aside the remaining budget surpluses in fiscal reserves, using the justification of providing a stronger buffer for future economic downturn and financial fluctuations. Statistics showed that the total amount of fiscal reserves held by the Hong Kong government have soared to a historical high level in recent years. As at 2012–2013, the amounts of fiscal reserves stood at HKD733.9 billion, which is equivalent to 36% of Hong Kong's nominal GDP or 23 months of government expenditure (Figs. 3.5 and 3.6). John Tsang had on many occasions rejected the idea of deploying fiscal reserves to finance

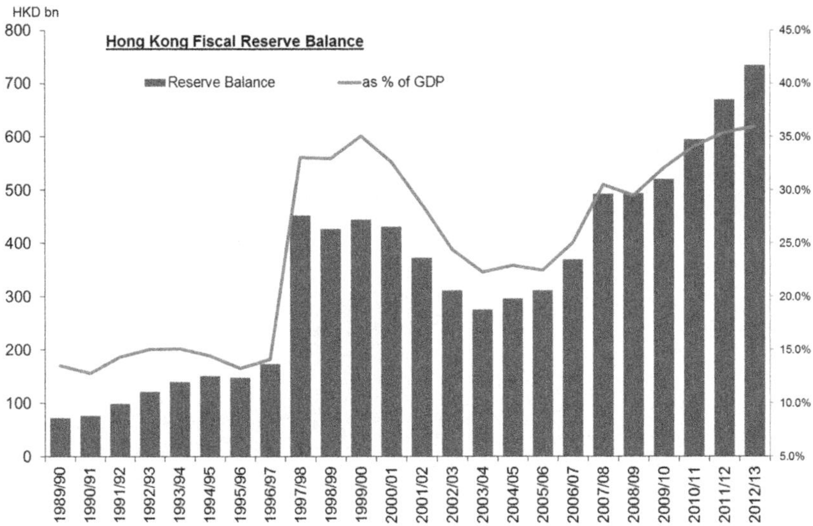

Fig. 3.5 Hong Kong government's fiscal reserves as percentage of nominal GDP (from 1989–1990 to 2012–2013). (Source: Author's own research based on the statistical tables available at the Census and Statistics Department's website at http://www.censtatd.gov.hk)

recurrent expenditure and defend his strategy of holding up the budget surpluses as reserves. For example, he once mentioned that:

> Some may think that the purpose of building up ample fiscal reserves is to provide a sufficient reserve capital for Hong Kong when our recurrent revenue is not sufficient to cover expenditure. I would say that this is not wrong but is a rather one-sided view. Of course, we can draw on our reserves to tackle short-term financial fluctuations. Yet fiscal reserves is not a regular revenue, it is all that we have at our disposal. The reserves can be exhausted. Prolonged depletion of the reserves to meet ever-increasing recurrent expenditure is not sustainable. Recurrent expenditure must be funded by sustainable revenue. (Hong Kong Special Administrative Region Government, 2013)

Unfortunately, John Tsang's budgetary strategy failed to win popular support and even backfire. Legislators across the political spectrum and

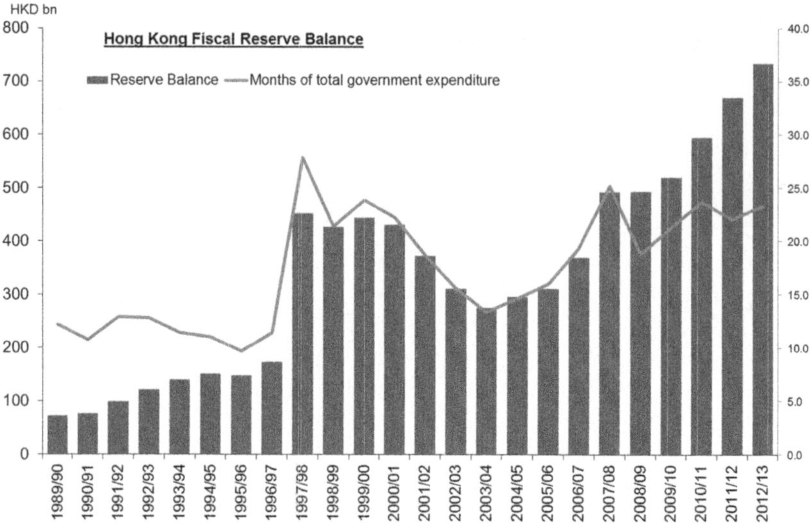

Fig. 3.6 Hong Kong government's fiscal reserves as months of government expenditure (from 1989–1990 to 2012–2013). (Source: Author's own research based on the statistical tables available at the Census and Statistics Department's website at http://www.censtatd.gov.hk)

major pressure groups have usually criticized Tsang as "lacking of vision and long-term planning" in budget allocation. John Tsang's strategy to implement one-off relief measures and to keep a high level of fiscal reserves was commonly seen by legislators and social activists as too "short-sighted" and "devoid of commitments." Critics usually argued that the budget surpluses and the massive fiscal reserves should better be spent on increasing recurrent expenditure items so that social services like education and welfare could be substantially improved.[7] The public resentment of the Financial Secretary's budgetary strategy was clearly reflected in the falling

[7] For example, the Hong Kong Council of Social Services, a leading social welfare group, in submitting their policy proposals for the 2011–2012 budget accused the Financial Secretary of lacking vision in alleviating the poverty problem and growing income polarization. They demanded that the Financial Secretary raise recurrent expenditure for improving welfare services such as the provision of comprehensive retirement benefits and a low-income subsidy instead of just giving out one-off sweeties (South China Morning Post, 2011). In a similar vein, the Hong Kong Professional Teachers Union, the most influential education union, criticized John Tsang for only handing out goodies but refusing to increase recurrent

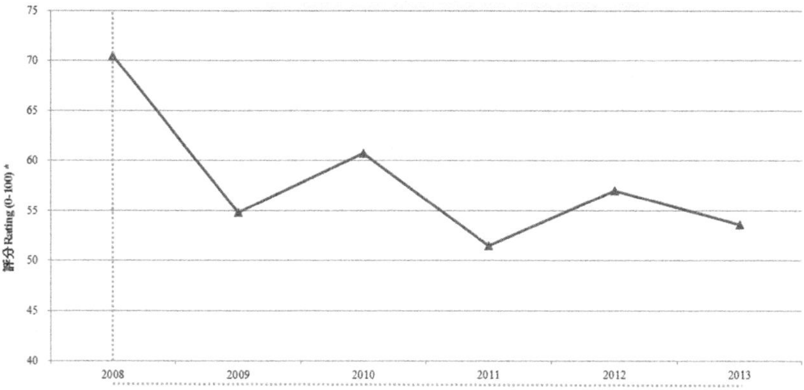

Fig. 3.7 Public ratings on John Tsang's Budget Speeches (from 2008–2009 to 2013–2014). (Source: The University of Hong Kong's Public Opinion Programme http://hkupop.hku.hk)

public ratings of his annual Budget Speeches, despite the handing out of billions of "one-off sweeties" (Fig. 3.7).

The accumulated public anger was finally erupted in the 2011–2012 budget. In anticipation of a huge budget surplus of HKD71.3 billion, John Tsang announced in the 2011–2012 Budget Speech to allocate a total of HKD24 billion to make a one-off injection of HKD6000 into the Mandatory Provident Fund (MPF) accounts of all working population.[8] Except for granting salaries tax rebates, John Tsang also announced other "one-off sweeties" such as waiving rates, paying extra allowance to recipients of Comprehensive Social Security Assistance and Old Age Allowance, waiving rental for public housing tenants, and providing electricity subsi-

expenditure on education, such as offering more young teachers long-term employment contracts (South China Morning Post, 2013).

[8] The Mandatory Provident Fund (MPF) System was implemented in December 2000 to provide a formal system of basic retirement protection for the working population in Hong Kong. The MPF system covers all employees who are at least 18 and under 65 years of age and under this system an employee and his/her employer are both statutorily required to contribute 5% of the employee's income as a mandatory contribution on a monthly basis. People are not allowed to draw the money from their MPF accounts until they reach the retirement age of 65. More information about the MPF system is available at: http://www.gov.hk/en/about/abouthk/factsheets/docs/mpf.pdf.

dy.[9] However, the billions of one-off measures announced by John Tsang had received more reproof than praise. Legislators across the political spectrum all criticized that the proposal of one-off injection of HKD6000 into each MPF account as too remote to be of any help because the general public were not allowed to draw the money until their retirement. Political parties were also dissatisfied with the Financial Secretary's decision to focus on handing out "one-off sweeties" instead of coming up with concrete long-term measures to address structural social problems (The Standard, 2011a). Opinion poll showed that over 41.3% of respondents were dissatisfied with the 2011–2012 budget and the public satisfaction rate stood only at 16.7%, indicating a marked increase in public resentment when compared with the previous budgets (The Standard, 2011b).

In view of the roaring public outcry, the pro-democracy parties called for a massive demonstration, labelled as the "Bauhinia Revolution," to voice their angers and grievances against John Tsang. Pro-democracy legislators also joined hands with their counterparts in the pro-regime camp to press the government for revising the budget. Initially, the Financial Secretary insisted that there was no room to revise or fine-tune the budget. But finally, as a result of the strong pressure of the pro-regime legislators, John Tsang announced substantial revisions to the 2011–2012 budget. First, instead of injecting money into every MPF accounts, the government will release a sum of HKD6000 cash to all Hong Kong permanent residents aged 18 or above; Second, a tax rebate of 75% of salaries tax will be offered to every tax payer, subject to a ceiling of HKD6000 (The Standard, 2011c).

The case of the 2011–2012 budget has clearly illustrated the challenges faced by the Financial Secretary when accommodating the competing demands of political parties, interest groups, and the general public. In particular, the case demonstrated how the Financial Secretary's budgetary proposals had been increasingly driven by partisan politics, through which legislators across the political spectrum made use of their veto power over the budget to press the government for policy concessions.

[9] Full text of the 2011–2012 Budget Speech is available at: https://www.budget.gov.hk/2011/eng/speech.html.

Conclusion

This chapter examines the Hong Kong budgetary decision-making from a historical perspective. It firstly highlights why and how the Financial Secretary dominated the budgetary decision-making under the traditional bureaucratic bargaining model in the pre-1980s period. Then it analyses how the internal and external driving forces both within and outside the Hong Kong government have transformed the budgetary decision-making into a model of pluralistic bargaining model since the 1980s–1990s.

Public budgeting is fundamentally a political process and it must be examined in the changing context of political systems, forces, and events. The changing models of Hong Kong's budgetary decision-making has proved once again why and how the political approach is central to the study and understanding of contemporary public budgeting.

Further Readings

- Yamamoto, K. (2018). Budgeting and Decision–Making. In A. Farazmand (Ed.), *Global Encyclopedia of Public Administration, Public Policy, and Governance* (pp. 476–483). Cham: Springer Nature.

An overview of the major theories of budgetary decision-making within the existing literature.

- Rubin, I. (2020). *The Politics of Public Budgeting: Getting and Spending, Borrowing and Balancing* (9th ed.). Thousand Oaks, CA; London: Sage/CQ Press.

One of the most popular texts on budgetary politics, analysing the major strands of the budgetary decision-making process.

- Lo, C. S. S. (1990). *Public Budgeting in Hong Kong: An Incremental Decision–making Approach*. Hong Kong: Writers' and Publishers' Cooperative.

The classical study of Hong Kong's budgetary decision-making in the pre-1990s period.

Bibliography

Cheung, A. B. L. (1998). The Transition of Bureaucratic Authority: The Political Role of the Senior Civil Service in the Post–1997 Governance of Hong Kong. In L. Pang-Kwong (Ed.), *Political Order and Power Transition in Hong Kong* (pp. 79–108). Chinese University Press.

Cheung, A. B. L. (2005). *Budgeting for Results or Budgeting for Politics: Budget Reforms, Fiscal Stability and Distributional Politics in Hong Kong Re-Examineds.* A Paper Presented in the 61st Congress of the International Institute of Public Finance Jeju, Korea, 22–25 August 2005.

Cheung, A. B. L. (2006). Budgetary Reforms in Two City States: Impact on the Central Budget Agency in Hong Kong and Singapore. *International Review of Administrative Sciences, 72*(3), 341–361.

Cheung, A. B. L. (2007). Executive-Led Governance or Executive Power 'Hollowed-Out' – The Political Quagmire of Hong Kong. *Asian Journal of Political Science, 15*(1), 17–38.

Chiu, S., & Wong, V. (2005). Hong Kong: From Familistic to Confucian Welfare. In A. Walker & C. K. Wong (Eds.), *East Asian Welfare Regimes in Transition: From Confucianism to Globalisation* (pp. 95–117). Policy Press.

Dawn.com. (2003). World Economic Report. 8 September. Retrieved June 5, 2021, from https://www.dawn.com/news/114259/world-economic-report

Fong, B. C. H. (2008). An Analysis of the 2003 'Zero-Three-Three' Civil Service Pay Reduction Settlement in Hong Kong: A Neopluralist Perspective. *Asian Profile, 36*(6), 559–580.

Fong, B. C. H. (2014). *Hong Kong's Governance Under Chinese Sovereignty: The Failure of the State-Business Alliance After 1997.* Routledge.

Fong, B. C. H. (2018). Executive-Legislative Disconnection in the HKSAR: The Erosion of the Legislative Support Base of the Chief Executives, 1997–2017. In B. C. H. Fong & T. L. Lui (Eds.), *Hong Kong: 20 Years After the Handover – Emerging Social and Institutional Fractures After 1997* (pp. 45–71). Palgrave Macmillan.

Harris, P. (1988). *Hong Kong: A Study in Bureaucratic Politics.* Heinemann Asia.

Hong Kong Special Administrative Region Government. (2002). Chief Executive's Remarks. Retrieved June 5, 2021, from https://www.info.gov.hk/gia/general/200212/07/1207155.htm

Hong Kong Special Administrative Region Government. (2003). Speech on the 2003–04 Budget delivered by the Financial Secretary. Retrieved June 5, 2021, from https://www.budget.gov.hk/2003/eng/budget.htm#The%20Size%20and%20Pay%20of%20the%20Civil%20Service

Hong Kong Special Administrative Region Government. (2011). Speech by the Financial Secretary on Second Reading Debate on Appropriation Bill 2011. Retrieved June 5, 2021, from http://www.info.gov.hk/gia/general/201104/13/p201104130221.htm

Hong Kong Special Administrative Region Government. (2013). Speech by the Financial Secretary on Second Reading Debate on Appropriation Bill 2013. Retrieved June 5, 2021, from http://www.info.gov.hk/gia/general/201302/27/p201302270241.htm

Khan, A. (2019). *Fundamentals of Public Budgeting and Finance*. Springer Nature.

Lau, S. K. (1982). *Society and Politics in Hong Kong*. Chinese University Press.

Lee, R. D., Johnson, R. W., & Joyce, P. B. (2013). *Public Budgeting Systems* (9th ed.). Jones & Bartlett Learning.

Lo, C. S. S. (1990). *Public Budgeting in Hong Kong: An Incremental Decision-Making Approach*. Writers' and Publishers' Cooperative.

Ma, N. (2007). *Political Development in Hong Kong: State, Political Society and Civil Society*. Hong Kong University Press.

Ma, N. (2012). Political Parties and Elections. In W. M. Lam, P. L. T. Lui, & W. Wong (Eds.), *Contemporary Hong Kong Government and Politics* (pp. 159–177). Hong Kong University Press.

Ma, N. (2020). China's Influence on Hong Kong's Elections: Evidence from Legislative Council Elections. In B. C. H. Fong, J. M. Wu, & A. J. Nathan (Eds.), *China's Influence and the Center-Periphery Tug of War in Hong Kong, Taiwan and Indo-Pacific* (pp. 91–104). Routledge.

Miners, N. (1998). *The Government and Politics of Hong Kong* (5th ed.). Oxford University Press.

Rabushka, A. (1976). *Value for Money: The Hong Kong Budgetary Process*. Hoover Institution Press.

Rabushka, A. (1979). *Hong Kong: A Study in Economic Freedom*. University of Chicago Press.

Rubin, I. (2020). *The Politics of Public Budgeting: Getting and Spending, Borrowing and Balancing* (9th ed.). Sage/CQ Press.

Scott, I. (2010). *The Public Sector in Hong Kong*. Hong Kong University Press.

South China Morning Post. (2011). Welfare Body Urges Long-Term Help for Needy. 14 February.

South China Morning Post. (2013). Legislators Want Tsang to Start Spending. 4 March.

Sung, Y. W., & Lee, M. K. (1991). *The Other Hong Kong Report*. Chinese University Press.

Tang, S. H. (1993). *Fiscal Legislation and Financial Control in Hong Kong (BRC Working Papers Series; ES 92031)*. Business Research Centre, Hong Kong Baptist College.

The Standard. (2011a). Miserly – That's How Legislators Describe It. 24 February.
The Standard. (2011b). Budget Cuts Popularity. 1 March.
The Standard. (2011c). $6,000 Cash in Hand. 3 March.
Wong, W. (2009). The Days After the End of the Asian Miracle: The Budget Crisis of Hong Kong. In S. Ming (Ed.), *Politics and Government in Hong Kong: Crisis Under Chinese Sovereignty* (pp. 136–161). Routledge.
Yamamoto, K. (2018). Budgeting and Decision-Making. In A. Farazmand (Ed.), *Global Encyclopedia of Public Administration, Public Policy, and Governance* (pp. 476–483). Springer Nature.

PART II

Comparative Analyses

CHAPTER 4

Budget Openness

This chapter compares whether and how budget openness in Hong Kong, Macao, and Taiwan is related to their regime trajectories.

In the comparative budgeting literature, the Open Budget Survey (OBS) is increasingly attracting prominence. Developed by the International Budget Partnership (IBP), an OBS-based comparative budgeting literature is being rapidly developed (De Renzio & Masud, 2011; Seifert et al., 2013). In this regard, existing OBS-based literature closely relates budget openness to democratization, arguing that the rise of competitive electoral and legislative politics will bring about improvement in budget openness at critical moments of democratization (Khagram et al., 2013).

Is this theory applicable to East Asian transitional regimes and to what extent? Hong Kong, Macao, and Taiwan, which are transitional regimes experiencing different regime trajectories, should be ideal places to test the validity of this theory. By examining whether and how open budget reforms in Hong Kong, Macao, and Taiwan are related to their regime

Originally published in a slightly different form under the title of "Democratization and Budget Openness: Evidences from Hong Kong, Macao, and Taiwan," reprinted from *International Review of Administrative Sciences*, 2019; 87(2), 311–327, by permission of SAGE Publications.

B. C. H. Fong, *Hong Kong Public Budgeting*, Hong Kong Studies Reader Series, https://doi.org/10.1007/978-981-16-5363-6_4

trajectories through historical-comparative case studies, this chapter aims to make an original contribution to the comparative budgeting literature by providing a new and unique set of OBS-based case studies in the context of East Asian transitional regimes.

Research Context

In recent decades, academics and international governmental organizations have taken an increasing interest in budget openness, arguing that disclosure of budgetary information to the public is conducive to good governance (Seifert et al., 2013). A body of empirical research was developed to demonstrate the positive consequences of budget openness for various governance outcomes, such as higher sovereign credit ratings, higher fiscal discipline, and better control over corruption (e.g. Reinikka & Jakob, 2004; Hameed, 2005; Glennerster & Yongseok, 2008).

The rising global interest in budget openness is evident by the development of systematic surveys and best practice manuals by different international governmental organizations such as the International Monetary Fund and the World Bank (Seifert et al., 2013). Among the various comparative measures of budget openness, the OBS has attracted considerable scholarly attention in recent years. Based on a standard questionnaire, the OBS measures the public availability of budgetary information in eight key budget documents,[1] the extent to which the public can participate in the budgetary process and the role of legislature and supreme audit institutions (International Budget Partnership, 2016). To facilitate cross-country comparisons across time, the IBP produced the Open Budget Index (OBI) by calculating a simple average of the quantified responses to the 95 questions relating to the budget discourse from the OBS questionnaire, assigning each country a score ranging from 0 to 100 (De Renzio & Masud, 2011).[2] In the latest 2019 OBS report, the average OBI score among 117 countries studied was 45 out of 100, with 20 countries disclosing scant budgetary information (OBI scores between 0 to 20), 30 countries releasing minimal budgetary information (OBI scores between 21 to 40),

[1] The eight key budget documents defined by the OBS questionnaire are the Pre-Budget Statement, Executive Budget Proposal and supporting documents, Citizens Budget, Enacted Budget, In-Year Report, Mid-Year Review, Year-End Report, and Audit Report (International Budget Partnership, 2016: 12–37).

[2] Open Budget Index Rankings: https://www.internationalbudget.org/open-budget-survey/open-budget-index-rankings.

36 countries providing limited budgetary information (OBI scores between 41 to 60), 25 countries publishing substantial budgetary information (OBI scores between 61 to 80), and 6 countries revealing extensive budgetary information (OBI scores between 81 to 100) (International Budget Partnership, 2020).

In recent years, an OBS-based comparative literature has been developed rapidly, focusing on investigating the determinants of the state of budget openness particularly on the causal effects of democratization. By adopting 2008 OBS data as a dependent variable and analysing its correlation with different measures of democracy, Wehner and de Renzio (2013) found that the "holding of free and fair elections" is positively correlated with the state of budget openness. This theory has been further illustrated by the country case studies of South Africa, Brazil, South Korea, Mexico, Guatemala, Tanzania, and Senegal, as covered by Khagram et al. (2013), who highlighted that the rise of competitive electoral and legislative politics at critical moments of democratization will result in improvement in budget openness, particularly when the democratic transitions were supplemented by the presence of reform-minded politicians, strong opposition parties, and organized civil society groups.

While *democratization* has been highlighted as the principal factor structuring the state of budget openness, other potential factors have also been discussed within the existing literature. In Khagram et al.'s (2013) country case studies, *fiscal/economic crises* are found to be significant in forcing governments to put in place new mechanisms for budgetary control and scrutiny, *corruption scandals* are viewed as effective in compelling governments to increase budget openness to pacify public discontent, and *external influences* from foreign donors and international agencies are considered conducive to budget openness. In Ríosa et al.'s (2013) statistical study, *Internet penetration* are regarded as significant in generating greater public demands for budget openness; furthermore, the *administrative tradition* matters, with Anglo-Saxon and Nordic countries disclosing more budgetary information than Continental countries, and *political ideology* is influential, with countries ruled by progressive parties having a higher degree of budget openness than countries ruled by conservative parties. Overall, different causal factors do not work in isolation but operate in different combinations and sequences to structure the trajectories of budget openness in different countries (Khagram et al., 2013).

Research Case Background

This chapter aims to examine whether and to what extent democratization has resulted in open budget reforms through comparative case studies of Hong Kong, Macao, and Taiwan. The reasons for choosing these three places are twofold.

First, the latest 2019 OBS report included 117 countries in its survey, and thus far it has not covered non-sovereign jurisdictions including Hong Kong, Macao, and Taiwan (International Budget Partnership, 2019). Constitutionally speaking, Hong Kong and Macao are "territorial autonomies" (Ghai & Woodman, 2013) while Taiwan is a "de facto regime" (Kaczorowska, 2010: 180). As far as the management of public finances is concerned the three places are all fiscally independent "primary governments" (Wang, 2014: 122) maintaining their own taxation systems and using all financial revenues for their own purposes. Therefore, by applying the OBS methodology to these three places, a new and important dataset can be developed to enrich the OBS-based literature.

Second, sharing a similar Chinese cultural orientation but currently situating at different stages of democratization, Hong Kong, Macao, and Taiwan should be ideal places to examine whether and how different types of transitional regimes undergo open budget reforms. Therefore, this chapter makes an important original contribution to enrich theory building on the determinants of budget openness.

In this section, I first provide the institutional backgrounds of the budgetary systems of these three transitional regimes.

Hong Kong: A Fiscally Autonomous Entity

Nicknamed the "Pearl of the Orient" during the British rule (1841–1997) and now officially called the Hong Kong Special Administrative Region (HKSAR) under the sovereignty of the People's Republic of China (PRC) (after 1997), Hong Kong has developed its fiscal autonomy for several decades (Goodstadt, 2010). Because running "the Empire on the cheap" was one of the governing principles of the British Empire (Brendon, 2007: 334), London imposed stringent fiscal discipline on all its colonies worldwide, including Hong Kong (Scott, 2010: 152). The annual budgets of Hong Kong's governments were required to be submitted to the Colonial Office for prior approval, and its foreign exchange reserves were also kept in London in the form of Sterling (Rabushka, 1976: 10 and 14). After the

Second World War, the disintegration of the British Empire resulted in an "informal devolution" of extensive autonomous powers from London to Hong Kong, including the powers to fully decide on its own annual budgets in 1958 and to manage its foreign exchange reserves in 1972 (Goodstadt, 2009: Chap. 3). The fiscal autonomous powers of Hong Kong were later codified by virtue of the *1984 Sino-British Joint Declaration* and the *1990 HKSAR Basic Law* as part of the "One Country Two Systems" (OCTS) model after the transfer of sovereignty from London to Beijing in 1997.

The *Public Finance Ordinance*, a local legislation enacted in 1983, stipulates the operation of the budgetary system and defines the roles of major budget actors, with the Financial Secretary being responsible for compiling annual budgets and the Legislative Council being responsible for scrutinizing and approving them. Both prior to and since 1997, the budgetary system remains broadly unchanged, although budgetary conflicts have become more prominent because of the rise of the Legislative Council as a partially elected chamber since the 1990s (Cheung, 2005; Ma, 2007: 111; Fong, 2015).

Macao: Another Fiscally Autonomous Entity

Similar to the case of Hong Kong, Macao gradually established its own fiscal autonomy during the period of Portuguese colonial rule (1557–1999), well before its transition into the Macao Special Administrative Region (MSAR) under the Chinese rule (after 1999). In 1583, a Senado composed of six elected representatives was established as a form of autonomous institutions governing the Portuguese community in Macao with tax collection authority. In 1783, such fiscal autonomous powers were absorbed by the Macao colonial government under the leadership of Portuguese Governors. In 1976, the *Organic Statute of Macao* was implemented by Lisbon, institutionalizing the fiscal autonomous powers of Macao, such as maintaining its own balance sheet, deciding on budgets, and collecting taxes (Liu & Su, 2013: 6–12). Modelled on the constitutional arrangements of Hong Kong, the *1987 Sino-Portuguese Joint Declaration* and the *1993 MSAR Basic Law* have constitutionally enshrined the fiscal independence of Macao under the OCTS model following the transfer of sovereignty from Lisbon to Beijing in 1999.

Currently, the structures and operation of Macao's budgetary system are governed by the *Framework Law of Budget*, with the Secretary of

Economy and Finance (with the support of the Finance Services Bureau) responsible for steering budget preparation, the MSAR Chief Executive announcing it as part of his annual policy addresses, and the MSAR Legislative Assembly scrutinizing and approving it.

Taiwan: A De Facto Regime with Full Fiscal Independence

When the Kuomintang (KMT) transplanted its regime from Mainland China to Taiwan after its defeat in the Chinese civil war by the Chinese Communist Party (CCP) in 1949, it effectively endowed Taiwan with "a de facto sovereign status in functional if not strictly legal terms" (Chu & Lin, 2001). Bearing the official name of the Republic of China (ROC), Taiwan is a de facto regime that effectively operates its own government and military forces, with its constitutional status being contested by the PRC.

As a de facto regime, Taiwan has exercised full-fledged fiscal independence. The *Budget Act* governs the compilation and implementation of the annual budgets of the ROC central government. The Directorate-General of Budget, Accounting and Statistics (under the leadership of the ROC Executive Yuan's Premier) functions as the central budget office, and the ROC Legislative Yuan acts as the budget approver.

Research Design

In the existing OBS-based literature, there are two major research approaches. The first approach is comparative statistical analysis, such as Wehner and de Renzio (2013) and Ross (2011), which develops correlation models for measuring the effects of certain causal factors on the level of budget openness. The second approach is historical-comparative case studies and the classical example is the volume edited by Khagram et al. (2013), which covers a total of eight country case studies. The choice of these two approaches depends on the research question and data availability. Comparative statistical analysis could provide us with interesting empirical patterns on the relationship between certain causal factors and the state of budget openness, but it "inevitably precludes a deeper investigation of what may have brought about changes in budget transparency over time" and usually fails to consider factors that "cannot be captured in statistical studies, such as the potential influence of civil society, political scandals or emerging international norms" (Khagram et al., 2013).

Because the principal research question that this chapter aims to address is whether and how budget openness in Hong Kong, Macao, and Taiwan are related to their democratization trajectories over several decades, instead of relying on comparative statistical analysis, I follow the historical-comparative case study approach of Khagram et al. (2013). This research approach will enable me to more deeply probe the extent to which democratization has shaped open budget reforms in Hong Kong, Macao, and Taiwan over a period of several decades through historical archives and data, without losing sight of other factors that cannot be captured by comparative statistical analysis (e.g. administrative tradition, corruption scandals, and Internet penetration).

Mapping the Regime Trajectories

Within the democratization literature, transitional regimes are defined as polities that experience "transitions away from autocratic rule" (Schmitter & Karl, 1991). Transition is not necessarily confined to "transition to democracy" but "transition to uncertain something else" (Merkel, 2011). In recent years, democratization literature increasingly theorized the latter case of transitional regimes as "hybrid regimes," referring to those democratizing regimes that do not follow a linear path towards full-democracy and stay in "grey zone" (Carothers, 2002). Conceptually, "transition" usually involves three stages, namely "liberalization" (the process of granting various liberal rights to citizens by the authoritarian government), "democratization" (the process of replacing the old repressive apparatus of the authoritarian regime with new democratic institutions), and "democratic consolidation" (the holding of the founding elections of the new democratic regime) (Merkel, 2011); and within this context, transitional regimes that successfully "transited to democracy" (democratic regimes) and currently "stay in grey zone" (hybrid regimes) could be considered as situating at different points of democratization.

Against this theoretical backdrop, Hong Kong, Macao, and Taiwan could be broadly conceptualized as transitional regimes with different regime trajectories. They all experienced transitions from authoritarian rule over the decades and are now situated at different stages of democratization. Hong Kong began its transition from authoritarian rule in the 1980s, but to date, it still stalls at the halfway point of the democratization stage, making it a *hybrid regime* (Ma, 2007: 226–227; Bush, 2016; Fong, 2016) featuring a partially democratized legislature and a quasi-appointed executive (Table 4.1).[3] Similarly, Macao began its transition from authoritarian rule in the 1970s and now it is still situated somewhere halfway in the democratization stage, making it another *hybrid regime* (Kwong & Wong, 2017; Kwong, 2017) featuring a partially democratized legislature and a quasi-appointed executive (Table 4.2).[4] Taiwan began its transition from authoritarian rule in the 1980s, and since then, it has gone through the stages of democratization and democratic consolidation, becoming a *democratic regime* (Fell, 2018: 33–49) with a fully democratized legislature (since 1992) and President (since 1996) (Table 4.3).

Studying the State of Budget Openness at Critical Moments of Democratization

To examine whether and to what extent democratization resulted in improvement in budget openness in Hong Kong, Macao, and Taiwan, I adopted a three-pronged approach to tracing the historical trajectories of budget openness of these three places in each of their critical moments of democratization. I first traced the state of budget openness of Hong Kong, Macao, and Taiwan "one year before" the introduction of any forms of popular/indirect elections (on the assumption that such financial years could be referenced as some form of "base years"). Then, I further traced the state of budget openness of the three places "three full years after" each critical moment of democratization (on the assumption that if that critical moment of democratization had resulted in open budget reforms, the implications of such reforms for budget openness could be fully reflected and tracked by the OBS questionnaire after three full years). Finally, I traced the state of budget openness of the three places in the "year of 2015" for contemporary comparison (Table 4.4).

The standard OBS methodology (International Budget Partnership, 2016) was consistently applied to all the financial years under study. Each

[3] Article 45 and 68 of the HKSAR Basic Law stipulated a democratization roadmap stating the "principle of gradual and orderly progress" and the "ultimate aim" of selecting the Chief Executive and all members of the Legislative Council by universal suffrage. But so far, Hong Kong still struggles to move towards the democratic regime as promised by the HKSAR Basic Law. For details, see Fong, 2016.

[4] Unlike HKSAR Basic Law, MSAR Basic Law does not mention universal suffrage as the "ultimate aim" of political reforms. Though, there are rising demands for democratization after the handover of Hong Kong usually cited as the reference point by Macao democrats. For details, see Zheng & Wan, 2014: 129–149.

Table 4.1 Partial democratization of Hong Kong's political regime

Legislative Council (from 1984 to present)

Session	*Number of seats chosen by popular elections*	*Number of seats chosen by indirect elections*	*Number of seats appointed by British Governors*	*Total number of seats*	*Percentage of seats chosen by popular elections*
1984–1985	0	0	61	61	0%
1985–1988	0	24	33	57	0%
1988–1991	0	26	33	59	0%
1991–1995	18	21	18	59	31%
1995–1997	20	40	0	60	33.33%
1998–2000	20	40	0	60	33.33%
2000–2004	24	36	0	60	40%
2004–2008	30	30	0	60	50%
2008–2012	30	30	0	60	50%
2012–2016	40[a]	30	0	70	57.14%
2016–2020	40[a]	30	0	70	57.14%

Governor/Chief Executive (from 1982 to present)

Tenure	*Name*	*Title*	*Selection process*
1982–1986	Edward Youde	Governor	Appointed by British monarch (on the advice of British government)
1987–1992	David Wilson	Governor	Appointed by British monarch (on the advice of British government)
1992–1997	Chris Patten	Governor	Appointed by British monarch (on the advice of British government)
1997–2002	Tung Chee-hwa	Chief Executive	Elected by a pro-Beijing 400-member Selection Committee and then appointed by Beijing
2002–2005	Tung Chee-hwa	Chief Executive	Elected by a pro-Beijing 400-member Selection Committee and then appointed by Beijing
2005–2007	Donald Tsang	Chief Executive	Elected by a pro-Beijing 400-member Selection Committee and then appointed by Beijing
2007–2012	Donald Tsang	Chief Executive	Elected by a pro-Beijing 800-member Election Committee and then appointed by Beijing
2012–2017	Leung Chun-ying	Chief Executive	Elected by a pro-Beijing 1200-member Election Committee and then appointed by Beijing
2017–2022	Carrie Lam	Chief Executive	Elected by a pro-Beijing 1200-member Election Committee and then appointed by Beijing

Source: Adapted from Ma, 2007 (for data before 1997); adapted from official data drawn from the Electoral Affairs Commission's website at https://www.eac.gov.hk (for data after 1997)

[a]Since 2012, on top of 35 direct election geographic constituency seats, 5 more new functional constituency seats have been introduced. The candidates for these 5 new functional constituency seats must be elected District Councillors, and they are chosen by all registered adult voters based on universal suffrage (with the whole of Hong Kong being organized as a single constituency). These 5 quasi-directly elected new functional constituency seats have been counted as "seats chosen by popular elections" together with the 35 direct election geographic constituency seats

Table 4.2 Partial-democratization of Macao's political regime

Legislative Assembly (from 1976 to present)

Session	*Number of seats chosen by popular elections*	*Number of seats chosen by indirect elections*	*Number of seats appointed by Portuguese Governors (before 1999) and Chief Executive (after 1999)*	*Total number of seats*	*Percentage of seats chosen by popular elections*
1976–1980	6	6	5	17	35%
1980–1984	6	6	5	17	35%
1984–1988	6	6	5	17	35%
1988–1992	8	8	7	23	35%
1992–1996	8	8	7	23	35%
1996–1999	8	8	7	23	35%
1999–2001	8	8	7	23	35%
2001–2005	10	10	7	27	37%
2005–2009	12	10	7	29	41%
2009–2013	12	10	7	29	41%
2013–2017	14	12	7	33	42.42%
2017–2022	14	12	7	33	42.42%

Governor/Chief Executive (from 1974 to present)

Tenure	*Name*	*Title*	*Selection process*
1974–1979	José Eduardo Martinho Garcia Leandro	Governor	Appointed by Portuguese President
1979–1981	Nuno Viriato Tavares de Melo Egídio	Governor	Appointed by Portuguese President
1981–1986	Vasco de Almeida e Costa	Governor	Appointed by Portuguese President
1986–1987	Joaquim Pinto Correia	Governor	Appointed by Portuguese President
1987–1991	Carlos Montez Melancia	Governor	Appointed by Portuguese President
1991–1999	Vasco Joaquim Rocha Vieira	Governor	Appointed by Portuguese President
1999–2004	Edmund Ho	Chief Executive	Elected by a pro-Beijing 200-member Selection Committee and then appointed by Beijing

(*continued*)

Table 4.2 (continued)

Governor/Chief Executive (from 1974 to present)			
Tenure	*Name*	*Title*	*Selection process*
2004–2009	Edmund Ho	Chief Executive	Elected by a pro-Beijing 300-member Election Committee and then appointed by Beijing
2009–2014	Fernando Chui	Chief Executive	Elected by a pro-Beijing 300-member Election Committee and then appointed by Beijing
2014–2019	Fernando Chui	Chief Executive	Elected by a pro-Beijing 400-member Election Committee and then appointed by Beijing

Source: Adapted from Lo, 2008, p. 48 (for data before 1999); adapted from official data drawn from the Chief Executive Electoral Affairs Commission's website at http://www.ece.gov.mo and the Legislative Assembly Electoral Affairs Commission's website at http://www.eal.gov.mo (for data after 1999)

Table 4.3 Democratization of Taiwan's political regime

Legislative Yuan (from 1989 to present)				
Session	*Number of seats chosen by popular elections*	*Number of seats chosen by methods other than popular elections*[a]	*Total number of seats*	*Percentage of seats chosen by popular elections*
1989–1992	79	204	283	28%
1993–1996	155	6	161	96%
1996–1999	158	6	164	96%
1999–2002	217	8	225	96%
2002–2005	217	8	225	96%
2005–2008	217	8	225	96%
2008–2012	107	6	113	95%
2012–2016	107	6	113	95%
2016–2020	107	6	113	95%

President (from 1978 to present)			
Tenure	*Name*	*Title*	*Selection process*
1978–1984	Chiang Ching-kuo	President	Elected by ROC National Assembly[b]
1984–1988	Chiang Ching-kuo	President	Elected by ROC National Assembly[b]
1988–1990	Lee Teng-hui	President	Succeeded to complete the remaining term of Chiang Ching-kuo after his death in 1988

(continued)

Table 4.3 (continued)

President (from 1978 to present)			
Tenure	*Name*	*Title*	*Selection process*
1990–1996	Lee Teng-hui	President	Elected by ROC National Assembly[b]
1996–2000	Lee Teng-hui	President	Elected by popular elections
2000–2004	Chen Shui-bian	President	Elected by popular elections
2004–2008	Chen Shui-bian	President	Elected by popular elections
2008–2012	Ma Ying-jeou	President	Elected by popular elections
2012–2016	Ma Ying-jeou	President	Elected by popular elections
2016–2020	Tsai Ing-wen	President	Elected by popular elections

Source: Adapted from Chang, 2010: 123; Chiu, 1994: 20; Fell, 2018: 50–71; Lasater, 1990: 24; Schafferer, 2003: 533–534 (for Taiwan's Legislative Yuan); adapted from official data drawn from the ROC Office of the President's website at https://english.president.gov.tw/Page/81 (for Taiwan's President)

[a]This category covers legislators who were chosen by methods other than popular elections, including a large number of retained seats dominated by Mainland Senior Parliamentarians (before 1992) and several seats reserved for overseas Chinese (1989–1992) and indigenous peoples (1989–2020)

[b]The ROC National Assembly, having functions such as electing the President/Vice-President and amending the constitution, was elected in 1947 in Mainland China before the KMT retreated to Taiwan. Subsequently, no full election was held, and the Mainland Senior Parliamentarians held their positions indefinitely, making the National Assembly nothing more than a rubber-stamping body for approving the decisions made by the KMT party-state during Taiwan's authoritarian era (Cooper, 1999)

OBS questionnaire was initially completed separately by two different field researchers, who substantiated each of the answer options that they chose with supporting evidence. Then, the two field researchers checked with one another to ensure that each of their answer options were consistent and, if necessary, to resolve their differences with concrete proofs. Finally, the OBI scores were compiled.

Research Findings and Discussion

The research findings indicated that the budget openness of Hong Kong, Macao, and Taiwan increased to varying degrees after most of the critical moments of democratization (Table 4.5). Such a pattern of findings conforms closely to the mainstream perspective of the existing OBS-based literature, highlighting the effects of democratization on improving the state of budget openness (e.g. Wehner & De Renzio, 2013; Khagram et al., 2013).

Table 4.4 Hong Kong, Macao, and Taiwan at critical moments of democratization

Hong Kong Note 1	1984-1985	1989-1990	1995-1996	2001-2002	2012-2013	2015-2016
Macao Note 2	1975	1980	1992	2003	2009	2015
Taiwan Note 3	1991-1992	1996-1997	2000	2004	2012	2015

denotes "liberalization/pre-democratization stage"

denotes "democratization stage"

denotes "democratic consolidation stage"

[1]"1984/85" was selected as the "base year," as it represents "one year before" the introduction of the first kind of election to the Legislative Council; "1989/90," "1995/96," "2001/02," and "2012/13" were selected to trace the state of budget openness of Hong Kong "three full years after" the introduction of 24 indirectly elected seats to the Legislative Council in 1985, the introduction of 18 directly elected seats to the Legislative Council in 1991, the transfer of sovereignty plus the introduction of indirect election to office of the Chief Executive in 1997, and the implementation of 30 directly elected seats to the Legislative Council as specified by Annex II of the HKSAR Basic Law in 2008, respectively. The financial year in Hong Kong starts on 1 April and ends on 31 March

[2]"1975" was selected as the "base year," as it represents "one year before" the introduction of the first kind of election to the Legislative Assembly; "1980," "1992," "2003," and "2009" were selected to trace the state of budget openness of Macao "three full years after" the introduction of 6 directly elected seats and 6 indirectly elected seats to the Legislative Assembly in 1976, the implementation of 8 directly elected seats and 8 indirectly elected seats to the Legislative Assembly in 1988, the transfer of sovereignty plus the introduction of indirect election to office of the Chief Executive in 1999, and the implementation of 12 directly elected seats to the Legislative Assembly as specified by Annex II of the MSAR Basic Law in 2005, respectively. The financial year in Macao starts on 1 January and ends on 31 December

[3]"1991/92" was selected as the "base year," as it represents "one year before" the introduction of full democratic election to the Legislative Yuan in 1992; "1996/97," "2000," "2004," and "2012" were selected to trace the state of budget openness of Taiwan "three full years after" the introduction of full democratic election to the Legislative Yuan in 1992, the introduction of full democratic election to the office of the President in 1996, the first power rotation in 2000, and the second power rotation in 2008, respectively. Prior to 1998, the financial year in Taiwan started on 1 July and ended on 30 June; since 1998, the financial year in Taiwan starts on 1 January and ends on 31 December

A closer examination of the findings provided us with more insights into the causal effects of democratization on structuring the budget openness of Hong Kong, Macao, and Taiwan over the decades.

In the case of Hong Kong, following the introduction of direct/indirect elections in the 1980s and 1990s, the Hong Kong government has become more prone to disclose budgetary information to the partially democratized Legislative Council in its annual budget cycles. Such changes

Table 4.5 OBI scores of Hong Kong, Macao, and Taiwan in the process of democratization

Hong Kong	1984-1985	1989-1990	1995-1996	2001-2002	2012-2013	2015-2016
	36.39	40.11	42.87	42.87	44.11	45.35
Macao	1975	1980	1992	2003	2009	2015
	12.34	13.26	18.52	35.17	40.71	44.1
Taiwan	1991-1992	1996-1997	2000	2004	2012	2015
	38.83	40.05	43.1	56.25	57.16	57.16

denotes "liberalization/pre-democratization stage"

denotes "democratization stage"

denotes "democratic consolidation stage"

have taken place against the backdrop of the transformation of the Legislative Council from an appointed chamber to a partially elected chamber in the 1980s and 1990s, with legislators of different party affiliations all becoming increasingly critical of the Hong Kong government over budgetary matters (Cheung, 2005; Ma, 2007: 111–112).[5] For example, it is an established practice for the Hong Kong government to finance expenditures on designated areas through several special government funds, and in 1984–1985 (and before), only the accounts of the Capital Works Reserve Fund were disclosed. However, it was recorded that as part of the legislative process of the annual Appropriation Bills, the Hong Kong government in 1989–1990 (and thereafter) disclosed the accounts of all special government funds in the "Budget Speech" delivered by the Financial Secretary and the "Government Estimates"; such broader disclosure resulted in corresponding improvements in the OBI scores (in terms of the "Executive Budget Proposal") in the financial year of 1989–1990. Similarly, it was recorded that in 1995–1996 (and thereaf-

[5] The stronger legislative oversight of the budgetary process was evident by the increasing number of written questions submitted by legislators in the Finance Committee of the Legislative Council during its deliberations on the annual budgets. Empirical research showed that the number of such questions kept increasing from approximately 1000 to over 5000 from 1999–2000 to 2012–2013; during the same period, the amount of time spent examining the annual budgets also increased from 28 days to 83 days. For details, see Yu, 2015, Chap. 4.

ter), after the announcement of the "Budget Speech" by the Financial Secretary in the Legislative Council, the Hong Kong government released a booklet called the "Introduction to the Estimates," aiming to provide legislators, reporters, and the public a handy reference. The information disclosure of this booklet has been refined in subsequent decades, resulting in corresponding improvements in the OBI scores (in terms of the "Citizen Budget") in the financial years of 1995–1996, 2001–2002, 2012–2013, and 2015–2016.

A similar story can be found in Macao. While it is generally accepted that the Macao Legislative Assembly and the democratic opposition are much less powerful than their counterparts in Hong Kong, the gradual introduction of direct/indirect elections since 1976 has subsequently consolidated the role of the Macao Legislative Assembly as a "competent political forum for the Macao polity" (Gonçalves, 2009), and in particular, after the handover, "the political pendulum is swinging from executive domination toward a greater role for the legislature" (Yu, 2011). Against this backdrop, over the decades, the Macao government has become prone to greater budgetary disclosure to the partially democratized Legislative Assembly in its annual budget cycles. For example, it was recorded that in 1975 (and before), the Macao government failed to disclose any budgetary information on government debt, borrowing, and contingent labilities in the "Government Budget Bill" submitted to the Legislative Assembly. However, it is recorded that in 1980 (and thereafter), the Macao government disclosed partial information about government debt and contingent liabilities, with such modest changes resulting in corresponding slight improvements in the OBI scores (in terms of the "Executive Budget Proposal") in the financial year of 1980. A more extensive budget disclosure was made to the Legislative Assembly through the annual "Government Budget Bills" and related legislative documents in subsequent decades, including the release of details about government expenditures (by different administrative, economic, and functional classifications) and government revenues (by different categories, sources, and years), thus resulting in corresponding substantial improvements in the OBI scores (in terms of the "Executive Budget Proposal") in the financial years of 1992, 2003, 2009, and 2015.

Compared with the partial democratization of Hong Kong and Macao, Taiwan experienced the most impressive open budget reforms during its transition to and consolidation as a full democratic regime (as opposed to Hong Kong and Macao's partially democratized hybrid regimes). Since the introduction of full democratic election to the Legislative Yuan in 1992, the Taiwanese government has made more budgetary disclosures to the Legislative Yuan in its annual budgeting process. Such changes have taken place against the backdrop of stronger legislsative oversight since the full democratization of the Legislative Yuan (Su, 2018). For example, it was recorded that in 1991–1992 (and before), the Taiwanese government failed to disclose the intergovernmental transfer estimates in the "Central Government General Budget Proposal" and provided limited data about the actual expenditures in the "Central Government Final Accounting." However, it was recorded in 1996–1997 (and thereafter) that the Taiwanese government provided more budget data about intergovernmental transfers in the "Central Government General Budget Proposal" and analysis on actual expenditures in the "Central Government Final Accounting," with such modest changes resulting in corresponding slight improvements in the OBI scores (in terms of the "Executive Budget Proposal" and "Year-End Report") in 1996–1997.

Further changes to budget disclosure were recorded in 2000, including the release of more details on government expenditures (by individual programmes and by different groups of citizens such as the elderly, women, youth, and indigenous peoples) in the "Central Government General Budget Proposal," reflecting substantial improvements in budget transparency implemented after the introduction of full democratic election to the office of the President in 1996. While there were modest improvements in the OBI scores in 2012 and 2015, the most obvious improvements in budget openness were recorded during the period of the first power rotation from 2000 to 2004, when President Chen Shui-bian of the Democratic Progressive Party (DPP) led the first non-KMT-led government in Taiwan's history. It was recorded that extensive budget disclosure had been introduced during this period, particularly about the comparisons between the original expenditure/revenue estimates and the actual expenditures/revenues in the "Central Government Final Accounting," the "Central Government General Budget Execution Report," and the "Central Government Half-Yearly Accounting." Such changes resulted in improvement almost across the board in different OBS indicators (in terms of the "Executive Budget Proposal," "Year-End Report," and "Mid-Year Review") in the financial year of 2004.

It is comprehensible that the growing powers and competences of the fully democratized Taiwan Legislative Yuan have played an important role in this process. Since 2000, the Legislative Budget Center (LBC) of the Legislative Yuan has been separated from the Legislative Consulting Office and empowered as a non-partisan budget think tank supporting the budget scrutiny work of legislators. With stronger professional staffing resources, the LBC actively publishes budget assessment reports that harshly criticize the government's expenditure efficiency, and such reports have attracted extensive public and media attention (Su, 2018).[6] Comparatively, until today no designated budget research offices have been set up in the legislatures of Hong Kong and Macao. Taiwan's journey towards open budget reforms, together with its impressive performance over Hong Kong and Macao in terms of the latest OBI scores in 2015, was the best illustration of the causal effects of democratization on budget openness.

Other Potential Explanations

While the causal effects of democratization on structuring the state of budget openness of Hong Kong, Macao, and Taiwan was obvious, as shown in the above empirical findings and analyses, it was the only factor shaping budget openness in these three places, and its effects should be qualified by other potential explanations.

For example, Hong Kong obtained a much higher OBI score than Macao in terms of their "base years" (36.39 vs. 12.34), meaning that when indirect/direct elections were completely absent in these two places, the state of budget openness of Hong Kong was still much better than that of Macao. It was comprehensible that the factor of administrative tradition was relevant in explaining such differences since Hong Kong, as a former British colony, had a long-established tradition of maintaining budget transparency for the scrutiny of the Colonial Office in London under the Colonial Regulations (Rabushka, 1976: 33–35). Additionally, the substantial improvement in the OBI scores of Macao during the 2003–2015 period (increasing from 35.17 to 44.1) was attributable to the factor of corruption scandals because the arrest of Secretary for Transport and Public Works Ao Man-long in 2006 and his conviction on several charges of corruption in 2008, 2009, and 2012 generated

[6] Up to 16 February 2019, the LBC has published a total of 4519 assessment reports on the Taiwan central government's budget estimates, accounts, and bills. See: https://www.ly.gov.tw/Pages/List.aspx?nodeid=6594.

public demand for a more transparent government in Macao (Zheng & Wan, 2014: 147). Finally, the superiority of the budget openness of Taiwan over that of Hong Kong and Macao (57.16 vs. 45.35 vs. 44.1) not only was the result of its full democratization but also was indicative of the importance of the factor of Internet penetration because, in terms of digital government, Taiwan is at the forefront globally (Institute of Digital Government, 2017).[7]

Of course, it is difficult to precisely quantify the relative weight of different causal factors over the changes of budget openness of Hong Kong, Macao, and Taiwan, but their experiences did validate Khagram et al. (2013)'s theory that democratization usually work together with different causal factors in structuring the state of budget openness.

Conclusion

This chapter is a pioneering attempt that applies the OBS methodology in the contexts of Hong Kong, Macao, and Taiwan through historical-comparative case studies. By studying their state of budget openness at their critical moments of democratization, this chapter finds that open budget reforms in Hong Kong, Macao, and Taiwan are related to their regime trajectories.

The OBS methodology provides budget scholars with a systematic, comparative measure for tracking the state of budget openness across the globe, but the interpretation and analysis of such data should be embedded within historical country case studies. Only by doing so can budget scholars make sense of the OBS figures and provide comprehensive qualitative accounts of the budget openness of countries and regions.

To date, however, Khagram et al. (2013) and this chapter are the only two major sets of historical country case studies on budget openness. Therefore, apart from extending the OBS methodology to more countries and regions, corresponding efforts should be made to enrich future OBS-based research with more historical-comparative case studies.

[7] Taiwan achieved a top-10 ranking globally in "Waseda-IAC international digital government ranking 2017 report" issued by the Institute of Digital Government. Under this survey, Hong Kong ranked 24th while Macao ranked 28th. For details, see the Institute of Digital Government, 2017.

Further Readings

- International Budget Partnership. (2019). *Guide to the Open Budget Questionnaire: An Explanation of the Questions and the Response Options*. Washington, DC. https://www.internationalbudget.org/sites/default/files/2020-04/2019_Guide_and_Questionnaire_EN.pdf

The latest version of OBS standard questionnaire, which provides an explanation of the 142 questions and the response options.

- International Budget Partnership. (2020). *Open Budget Survey 2019*. Washington, DC. https://www.internationalbudget.org/open-budget-survey/open-budget-survey-2019

The latest, seventh OBS report, which assessed and compared the state of budgetary openness, public participation, and oversight in 117 countries.

- Khagram, S., Fung, A., & De Renzio, P. (Eds.). *Open Budgets: The Political Economy of Transparency, Participation, and Accountability*. Baltimore, MD: Project MUSE.

The most comprehensive account of the causes and consequences of budget openness based on OBS datasets. It covers a total of eight in-depth country case studies on South Africa, Brazil, South Korea, Mexico, Guatemala, Tanzania, Vietnam, and Senegal.

Bibliography

Brendon, P. (2007). *The Decline and Fall of the British Empire 1781–1997*. Jonathan Cape Bright.

Bush, R. C. (2016). *Hong Kong in the Shadow of China: Living with the Leviathan*. Brookings Institution Press.

Carothers, T. (2002). The End of the Transition Paradigm. *Journal of Democracy, 13*(1), 5–21.

Chang, S. H. (2010). *From Years Congress to Comprehensive Re-Election: One Aspect of the Democratization Process in Taiwan*. M.phil. Dissertation, National Chengchi University, Taiwan.

Cheung, A. B. L. (2005). *Budgeting for Results or Budgeting for Politics: Budget Reforms, Fiscal Stability and Distributional Politics in Hong Kong Re-Examineds.* A Paper Presented in the 61st Congress of the International Institute of Public Finance Jeju, Korea, 22–25 August 2005.

Chiu, H. (1994). Constitutional Development and Reform in the Republic of China on Taiwan. In B. Lin & J. T. Myers (Eds.), *Contemporary China and the Changing International Community* (pp. 3–34). University of South California.

Chu, Y. H., & Lin, J. W. (2001). Political Development in Twentieth-Century Taiwan: State-Building, Regime Transformation and the Construction of National Identity. In R. L. Edmonds & S. M. Goldstein (Eds.), *Taiwan in the Twentieth Century: A Retrospective View* (pp. 102–129). Cambridge University Press.

Cooper, J. F. (1999). *Taiwan: Nation-State or Province?* (3rd ed.). Westview Press.

De Renzio, P., & Masud, H. (2011). Measuring and Promoting Budget Transparency: The Open Budget Index as a Research and Advocacy Tool. *Governance, S1*, 607–616.

Fell, D. (2018). *Government and Politics in Taiwan.* Routledge.

Fong, B. C. H. (2015). The Politics of Budget Surpluses: The Case of China's HKSAR. *International Review of Administrative Sciences, 81*(1), 134–157.

Fong, B. C. H. (2016). In-Between Liberal Authoritarianism and Electoral Authoritarianism: Hong Kong's Democratization Under Chinese Sovereignty, 1997–2016. *Democratization, 24*(4), 724–750.

Ghai, Y. P., & Woodman, S. (2013). *Practising Self-Government: A Comparative Study of Autonomous Regions.* Cambridge University Press.

Glennerster, R., & Yongseok, S. (2008). Does Transparency Pay? *IMF Staff Papers, 55*(1), 183–209.

Gonçalves, A. M. A. (2009). Macau's Autonomy: Looking for a Fresh Awakening? In J. C. Oliveira & P. Cardinal (Eds.), *One Country, Two Systems, Three Legal Orders: Perspectives of Evolution, Essays on Macau's Legal Status After the Resumption of Sovereignty by China* (pp. 733–740). Springer.

Goodstadt, L. F. (2009). *Uneasy Partners: The Conflict Between Public Interest and Private Profit Interest in Hong Kong.* Hong Kong University Press.

Goodstadt, L. F. (2010). Fiscal Freedom and the Making of Hong Kong's Capitalist Society. *China Information, 24*(3), 273–294.

Hameed, F. (2005). *Fiscal Transparency and Economic Outcomes.* IMF Working Paper (WP/05/225). Washington, International Monetary Fund.

Institute of Digital Government. (2017). *Waseda-IAC International Digital Government Ranking 2017 Report.* Tokyo, Japan. http://iacio.org/pdf/2017_digital-government_ranking_press_release.pdf

International Budget Partnership. (2016). *Guide to the Open Budget Questionnaire: An Explanation of the Questions and the Response Options.* Washington. https://www.internationalbudget.org/wp-content/uploads/open-budget-survey-2017-guide-andquestionnaire-english.pdf

International Budget Partnership. (2019). *Guide to the Open Budget Questionnaire: An Explanation of the Questions and the Response Options.* Washington, DC. Retrieved February 3, 2021, from https://www.internationalbudget.org/sites/default/files/2020-04/2019_Guide_and_Questionnaire_EN.pdf

International Budget Partnership. (2020). *Open Budget Survey 2019.* Washington, DC. Retrieved February 3, 2021, from https://www.internationalbudget.org/open-budget-survey/open-budget-survey-2019

Kaczorowska, A. (2010). *Public International Law* (4th edition). Abingdon: Routledge.

Khagram, S., De Renzio, P., & Fung, A. (2013). Overview and Synthesis: The Political Economy of Fiscal Transparency, Participation, and Accountability Around the World. In S. Khagram, A. Fung, & P. De Renzio (Eds.), *Open Budgets: The Political Economy of Transparency, Participation, and Accountability* (pp. 1–50). Project MUSE.

Kwong, Y. H. (2017). Ruling Coalition Restructuring under Macao's Hybrid Regime. *China Review, 173*(3), 111–139.

Kwong, Y. H., & Wong, M. Y. H. (2017). State Size and Democratization in Hybrid Regimes: The Chinese Island Cities of Macau and Hong Kong. *Island Studies Journal, 12*(2), 113–126.

Lasater, M. L. (1990). *A Step Toward Democracy – The December 1989 Election in Taiwan, ROC.* AEI Press.

Liu, Z., & Su, Z. (2013). *Aomen Yu Xianggang Cai Zheng Zheng Ce Bi Jiao Yan Jiu [澳門與香港財政政策比較研究].* Aomen Jing Ji Xue Hui (In Chinese).

Lo, S. S. H. (2008). *Political Change in Macau.* Routledge.

Ma, N. (2007). *Political Development in Hong Kong: State, Political Society and Civil Society.* Hong Kong University Press.

Merkel, W. (2011). Transition. In B. Badie, D. Berg-Schlosser, & L. Morlino (Eds.), *International Encyclopedia of Political Science* (pp. 2661–2663). SAGE Publications.

Rabushka, A. (1976). *Value for Money: The Hong Kong Budgetary Process.* Hoover Institution Press.

Reinikka, R., & Jakob, S. (2004). *The Power of Information: Evidence from a Newspaper Campaign to Reduce Capture (Policy Research Working Paper 3239).* World Bank.

Ríosa, A. M., Benito, B., & Bastida, F. (2013). Determinants of Central Government Budget Disclosure: An International Comparative Analysis. *Journal of Comparative Policy Analysis: Research and Practice, 15*(3), 235–254.

Ross, M. (2011). *Mineral wealth and budget transparency.* IBP Working Paper 2. Washington, International Budget Partnership.

Schafferer, C. (2003). The Legislative Yuan Election, Taiwan 2001. *Electoral Studies, 22*(3), 532–537.

Schmitter, P. C., & Karl, T. L. (1991). What Democracy is … and is Not. *Journal of Democracy, 2*(3), 75–88.

Scott, I. (2010). *The Public Sector in Hong Kong*. Hong Kong University Press.
Seifert, J., Carlitz, R., & Mondo, E. (2013). The Open Budget Index (OBS) as a Comparative Statistical Tool. *Journal of Comparative Policy Analysis: Research and Practice, 15*(1), 87–101.
Su, T. T. (2018). Public Budgeting System in Taiwan: Does it Lead to Better Value for Money? In A. Podger, T. T. Su, & J. Wanna (Eds.), *Value for Money: Budget and Financial Management Reform in the People's Republic of China* (pp. 79–93). Australian National University.
Wang, X. H. (2014). *Financial Management in the Public Sector: Tools, Applications, and Cases* (3rd ed.). M.E. Sharpe, Inc.
Wehner, J., & De Renzio, P. (2013). Citizens, Legislators, and Executive Disclosure: The Political Determinants of Fiscal Transparency. *World Development, 41*, 96–108.
Yu, E. W. Y. (2011). Executive-Legislature Relationships and the Development of Public Policy. In L. Newman & I. Scott (Eds.), *Gaming, Governance and Public Policy in Macao* (pp. 57–64). Hong Kong University Press.
Yu, G. (2015). *Hong Kong's Legislature Under China's Sovereignty, 1998–2013*. Brill Nijhoff.
Zheng, V., & Wan, P. S. (2014). *Gambling Dynamism: The Macao Miracle*. Springer.

CHAPTER 5

Budget Oversight

This chapter compares the budget oversight institutions and practices in Hong Kong and Macao.

Traditionally, comparative budgeting scholars have focused on analysing budget oversight at the sovereign state level. Over the years, several researchers have developed comparative indices to examine the budget oversight operations of institutions worldwide (Wehner, 2006; Santiso, 2009; International Budget Partnership, 2020). However, the nature and characteristics of budget oversight in non-sovereign jurisdictions, particularly in territorial autonomies with extensive fiscal powers, remains unclear.

Given the growing role of territorial autonomies in managing their own public finances, this chapter aims to address this hitherto under-explored research area through a comparative study of Hong Kong and Macao. It is a pioneering attempt to compare the budget oversight institutions and practices in Hong Kong and Macao under the "One Country Two Systems" (OCTS) model. This chapter will demonstrate that the varying practices of budget oversight of Hong Kong and Macao are the

Originally published in a slightly different form under the title of "Budget Oversight in Territorial Autonomies: A Comparative Analysis of Hong Kong and Macao," reprinted from *International Review of Administrative Sciences*, Article first published online: 11 August 2021, https://doi.org/10.1177/00208523211033816, by permission of SAGE Publications.

B. C. H. Fong, *Hong Kong Public Budgeting*, Hong Kong Studies Reader Series, https://doi.org/10.1007/978-981-16-5363-6_5

consequences of their different bases of opposition politics, including democratic opposition, the media, and the civil society.

Research Context

Public budgeting is primarily concerned with the use of public resources, a process which necessitates a great degree of accountability. Therefore, budget oversight or the institutions and activities designed to hold the government accountable to the legislature and the supreme audit institution (SAI) throughout the different stages of the budget cycle (Warner, 2018) are commonly regarded as an important component of good governance. Recently, budget oversight has been promoted by international organizations, such as the United Nations (UN), the International Monetary Fund (IMF), and the Organization for Economic Co-operation and Development (OECD), particularly during the COVID-19 pandemic (United Nations, 2017: 134–143; International Monetary Fund, 2020; Organization for Economic Co-operation and Development, 2020). Over time, the importance of budget oversight, both theoretical and practical, has driven the global comparative budgeting scholarship to investigate and compare the budget oversight process across different states, using several systematic comparative tools and indices. However, all existing comparative indices adopt a state-centric perspective and study budget oversight only at the sovereign state level.

Wehner (2006) used a survey of budgeting procedures and developed an index to compare the legislative oversight of 36 democratic countries. He assessed the legislature's oversight functions against six institutional benchmarks, namely, amendment powers, reversionary budgets, executive flexibility at the implementation stage, the timing of the budgets, legislative committee systems, and budgetary information. Santiso (2009) devised a quantitative index to assess the political economy of budget oversight in 10 Latin American countries, based on the parameters of authentication, authorization, and accounting. The International Budget Partnership's (IBP) comprehensive, fact-based comparative tool, the Open Budget Survey (OBS) has been an effective instrument in assessing public budgeting quality since 2006. Based on a standard questionnaire of 145 questions, the OBS measures three major dimensions of public budgeting practices worldwide—transparency, participation, and oversight. As far as budget oversight is concerned, the OBS "examines the role that legislatures and supreme audit institutions play in the budget process and the extent to which they can provide robust oversight of the budget" (International Budget Partnership, 2021). In its latest report, the IBP found that only 30 out of the 117 countries surveyed attained adequate scores in both legislative and SAI oversight—a majority of legislatures presented rubber-stamp budgets without amendments and exercised limited monitoring in budget execution, while most SAIs were quite powerless in ensuring government response to their audit recommendations (IBP, 2020: 60–63).

While the existing literature provides extensive comparative analyses of budget oversight at the sovereign state level, there are lacunae in budget oversight research at the sub-state jurisdiction level. To address these gaps, this chapter examines how budget oversight operates at the territorial autonomy level, where different degrees of fiscal autonomous powers have been granted by the centre. A survey of territorial autonomies worldwide showed that they may be granted either a certain degree of taxation and spending powers for specified areas, such as the cases of the Åland Islands, Catalonia, Jammu and Kashmir, Norfolk Island, and Quebec, or almost full-fledged fiscal autonomy, such as in Hong Kong, Macao, Puerto Rico, and South Tyrol (Ghai & Woodman, 2013). There are, however, few systematic studies and little consensus regarding budget oversight practices of territorial autonomies worldwide.

This chapter is a pioneering attempt to establish a more comprehensive understanding of budget oversight, not just at the sovereign state but also at the sub-state level, through a comparative study of Hong Kong and Macao. It endeavours to contribute to the existing comparative budgeting literature by broadening the research focus from sovereign states to territorial autonomies.

Research Case Background

Most-Similar-System Comparison of Hong Kong and Macao

This study adopts a "most-similar-system" research design strategy by selecting Hong Kong and Macao, two territorial autonomies under the "One Country Two Systems" (OCTS) model, as binary cases. Broadly speaking, Hong Kong and Macao are similar in many important dimensions, including their autonomist arrangements (the OCTS model), historical backgrounds (former Western colonies), socio-economic structures (wealthy global cities), population composition (predominantly Chinese societies with a proportion of non-Chinese minorities), and culture (hybrid East–West culture).

To use the words of comparative scholars (Hague & Harrop, 2013: 368; Peters, 2013: 39–44), the high degree of similarities between Hong Kong and Macao effectively controls for extraneous difference and helps identify the potential factors that shape the different trajectories of budget oversight. A "most-similar-system" research approach is thus particularly suitable for the present exploratory comparative study of budget oversight at territorial autonomy level.

Fiscal Autonomy and Oversight Institutions in Hong Kong and Macao

After Britain and Portugal handed over their sovereignty to China in 1997 and 1999, respectively, both Hong Kong and Macao operate as territorial autonomies, officially termed Special Administrative Regions (SARs) under the OCTS model. Both the Hong Kong and Macao governments were constitutionally granted full-fledged fiscal autonomy, including the autonomous power to formulate budgets, maintain independent taxation systems, retain all financial revenues exclusively for their own spending, and manage and control their own fiscal reserves.[1] In practice, the offices of Financial Secretaries in Hong Kong and the Secretaries for Economy and Finance in Macao are respectively the central budgeting agencies of the two SARs, practically exercising all autonomous fiscal powers, including budget compilation, overseeing budget execution, and managing fiscal reserves.

Owing to their similar fiscal autonomous systems, prima facie, both Hong Kong and Macao operate similar budget oversight institutions under the SARs Basic Laws. In terms of legislative oversight, both the Legislative Council in Hong Kong[2] and the Legislative Assembly in

[1] For the full text of the HKSAR Basic Law, see: https://www.basiclaw.gov.hk; for the full text of the MSAR Basic Law, see: https://bo.io.gov.mo/bo/i/1999/leibasica (available in Chinese and Portuguese only).

[2] The partial-democratisation of Hong Kong's Legislative Council began in 1991 when 18 directly-elected seats were added to the 60-member legislature. Direct election elements have been gradually increased to nearly 60% since 2012, including the five new quasi-directly elected, functional constituencies of "super district councillors." For an account, see Ma (2012).

Macao[3] underwent partial-democratization in the final decades of their colonial rule, with such a partially democratic composition codified into the Basic Laws after the handover. The legislatures in both Hong Kong and Macao are empowered by their Basic Laws to examine and approve government budgets. In terms of SAI oversight, both the Audit Commission in Hong Kong and the Commission of Audit in Macao are empowered by the Basic Laws to "function independently."

Notwithstanding these powers, the legislatures and SAIs in Hong Kong and Macao are not constitutionally designed to act as full-fledged oversight institutions such as in Western democracies.[4] Their powers and functions to monitor government budgets have been constitutionally constrained by certain provisions of the Basic Laws; for example, members of both legislatures are prohibited from introducing any bills related to "public expenditure"; the Basic Laws also define both Directors of Audit as principal officials who are nominated by and are accountable to the Chief Executives for Beijing's appointments (rather than to the legislatures). Such constitutional constraints reflect Beijing's preferences for putting in place "executive-dominant governments" in Hong Kong and Macao (Chou, 2013).

Tables 5.1 and 5.2 summarize the similar sets of budget oversight institutions that have been put in place for the Hong Kong and MSARs as part of their fiscal autonomous regimes under the OCTS model (Tables 5.1 and 5.2).

Research Design

Instead of following the methodology and comparative tools of Wehner (2006) and Santiso (2009), this study adopted the standard OBS methodology to compare the state of budget oversight in Hong Kong and Macao. This research design was used for two major reasons. First, the OBS methodology is the most comprehensive measurement tool to have been developed so far, covering not only budget oversight, but also budget transparency and participation. For many years, how to measure budget

[3] The partial-democratization of Macao's Legislative Council began in 1976, with about one-third of directly elected seats added to the 17-member legislature. Direct election elements have been gradually increased to more than 40% since 2013. For an account, see Yu (2011).

[4] For general accounts of budgetary and legislative politics of Hong Kong and Macao, see Fong (2015, 2018) and Yu (2011) respectively.

Table 5.1 Fiscal autonomous powers of Hong Kong and Macao

	Hong Kong	*Macao*
Devolution of fiscal autonomous powers		
Formulating budgets	HKSAR Basic Law Article 62(4): "The Government of the Hong Kong Special Administrative Region shall exercise the following powers and functions: ... (4) To draw up and introduce budgets and final accounts;"	MSAR Basic Law Article 64(4): "The Government of the Macao Special Administrative Region shall exercise the following powers and functions: ... To draw up and introduce budgets and final accounts;"
Spending	HKSAR Basic Law Article 106: "Hong Kong Special Administrative Region shall have independent finances. The Hong Kong Special Administrative Region shall use its financial revenues exclusively for its own purposes, and they shall not be handed over to the Central People's Government."	MSAR Basic Law Article 104: "The Macao Special Administrative Region shall have independent finances. All the financial revenues of the Macao Special Administrative Region shall be managed and controlled by the Region itself and shall not be handed over to the Central People's Government."
Taxation	HKSAR Basic Law Article 106: "The Central People's Government shall not levy taxes in the Hong Kong Special Administrative Region." HKSAR Basic Law Article 108: "The Hong Kong Special Administrative Region shall practise an independent taxation system."	MSAR Basic Law Article 104: "The Central People's Government shall not levy taxes in the Macao Special Administrative Region." MSAR Basic Law Article 106: "The Macao Special Administrative Region shall practise an independent taxation system."
Managing reserves	HKSAR Basic Law Article 113: "The Exchange Fund of the Hong Kong Special Administrative Region shall be managed and controlled by the government of the Region, primarily for regulating the exchange value of the Hong Kong dollar."	MSAR Basic Law Article 109: "The foreign exchange reserve of the Macao Special Administrative Region shall be managed and controlled by the Government of the Macao Special Administrative Region according to law."
Exercise of fiscal autonomous powers		
Central budgeting agency	The office of Financial Secretaries, among its other duties, oversees the government budgeting of the HKSAR, including laying, before the Legislative Council each year, the annual estimates of government revenue and expenditure.	The office of Secretaries for Economy and Finance, among its other duties, plans, coordinates, and oversees public budgeting activities of the MSAR.

Table 5.2 Budget oversight institutions of Hong Kong and Macao

	Hong Kong	*Macao*
Legislative oversight		
Powers and functions	HKSAR Basic Law Article 73(2) and (3): "The Legislative Council of the Hong Kong Special Administrative Region shall exercise the following powers and functions: ... (2) To examine and approve budgets introduced by the government; (3) To approve taxation and public expenditure;"	MSAR Basic Law Article 71(2) and (3): "The Legislative Council of the Macao Special Administrative Region shall exercise the following powers and functions: ... (2) To examine and approve budgets introduced by the government; and examine the report on audit introduced by the government; (3) To decide on taxation according to government motions and approve debts to be undertaken by the government;"
Constraints	HKSAR Basic Law Article 74: "Bills which do not relate to public expenditure or political structure or the operation of the government may be introduced individually or jointly by members of the Council."	MSAR Basic Law Article 75: "Bills which do not relate to public expenditure or political structure or the operation of the government may be introduced individually or jointly by members of the Council."
SAI oversight		
Powers and functions	HKSAR Basic Law Article 58: "A Commission of Audit shall be established in the Hong Kong Special Administrative Region. It shall function independently and be accountable to the Chief Executive."	MSAR Basic Law Article 60: "A Commission of Audit shall be established in the Macao Special Administrative Region. It shall function independently, and its Director shall be accountable to the Chief Executive."

(*continued*)

Table 5.2 (continued)

	Hong Kong	*Macao*
Constraints	HKSAR Basic Law Article 48(5): "The Chief Executive of the Hong Kong Special Administrative Region shall exercise the following powers and functions: ... (5) To nominate and to report to the Central People's Government for appointment the following principal officials: Secretaries and Deputy Secretaries of Departments, Directors of Bureaux, Commissioner Against Corruption, Director of Audit, Commissioner of Police, Director of Immigration and Commissioner of Customs and Excise; and to recommend to the Central People's Government the removal of the above-mentioned officials;"	MSAR Basic Law Article 50(6): "The Chief Executive of the Macao Special Administrative Region shall exercise the following powers and functions: ... (6) To nominate and to report to the Central People's Government for appointment the following principal officials: Secretaries of Departments, Commissioner against Corruptions, Director of Audit, the leading members of the Police and the customs and excise; and to recommend to the Central People's Government the removal of the above-mentioned officials"

transparency and oversight, which are "fundamentally important, but elusive" (Heald, 2012: 30), is always a methodological challenge to comparative budgeting scholars. In recent years, the OBS methodology emerges to fill this gap, with a cross-country dataset and an OBS-based scholarly literature rapidly developed (De Renzio & Masud, 2011; Seifert et al., 2013). Therefore, by applying the OBS methodology, this study has much greater theoretical potential and applicability for public budgeting studies. Second, the OBS methodology has been extensively applied to different contexts, both geographically (117 countries) as well as temporally (from 2006 to 2019). In applying the OBS methodology to Hong Kong and Macao, this study may potentially be extended by future researchers to explore territorial autonomies worldwide and merged with the existing sovereign state-centric OBS database, therefore generating comparative budgeting observational datasets for multi-level jurisdictions.

This study adopted the latest version of the OBS standard questionnaire (International Budget Partnership, 2019), comprising 145 questions covering three dimensions—budget transparency (109 questions), budget participation (18 questions), and budget oversight (18 questions). For the purpose of this study, only OBS Questions 107–124, the 18 questions directly related to budget oversight, were used to measure the evolution of legislative and SAI oversight in Hong Kong and Macao over the decades. These questions assess the role and effectiveness of budget oversight institutions by a number of yardsticks, such as the scope of legislative authority to amend government budgets, the availability of a specialized finance committee to examine government budgets, the power of the government to reallocate funds between administrative units, the role of legislative committees in examining the SAI audit reports, the appointment and removal of the SAI head, the power of the SAI to undertake independent audits, and the frequency with which the SAI officials testify in legislative committee hearings (International Budget Partnership, 2019: 117–134).

This study surveyed the post-handover state of budget oversight from the first budgets for the Hong Kong and MSARs (1998–1999 and 2000, respectively) up to fiscal year 2019.[5] Following the OBS methodology, all 18 questions on budget oversight were answered by choosing one out of five responses—"a" ("the standard is fully met"), "b" ("the basic elements of the standard have been met or largely met"), "c" ("minimal efforts have been made to attain the relevant standard"), "d" ("the standard is not met at all"), and "e" ("the standard is not applicable"). Three different scores, namely, "composite budget oversight" (OBS Questions 107–124), "legislative oversight" (OBS Questions 107–117), and "SAI oversight" (OBS Questions 118–124), were quantified for each fiscal year by averaging the relevant numeric scores, that is, 100 for "a," 67 for "b," 33 for "c," 0 for "d," and "e" being excluded from the calculation (International Budget Partnership, 2019: 6–7).

Research Findings and Discussion

Research Findings: Similar Oversight Institutions, Different Oversight Practices

The findings indicated that Hong Kong's "composite budget oversight" scores (averaging 28.6) were consistently well above Macao's (averaging 13.7) throughout the post-handover period (OBS Questions 107–124) (Fig. 5.1). This empirical pattern implies that the Hong Kong

[5] Hong Kong's annual budget covers the period between 1 April to 31 March, while the annual budget of Macao covers the period from 1 January to 31 December.

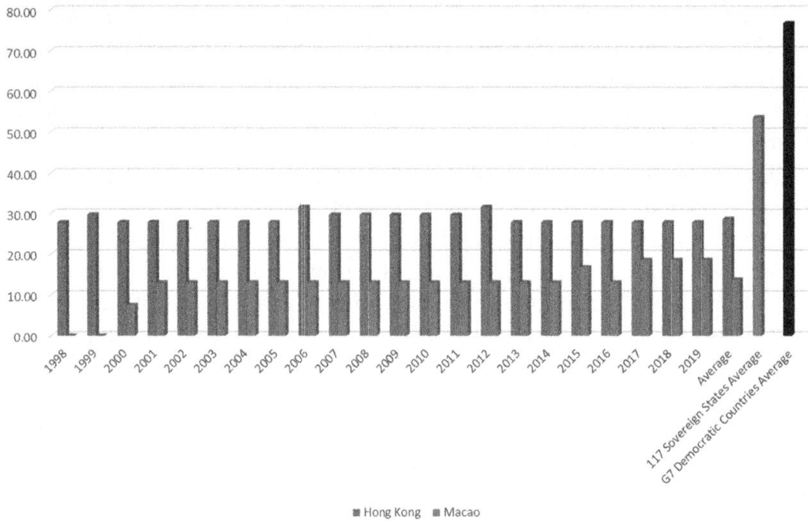

Fig. 5.1 Post-handover composite budget oversight scores for Hong Kong and Macao. (Note: Each fiscal year's score was quantified by averaging the scores attained by Hong Kong and Macao on Questions 107–124 (all OBS questions on budget oversight), the highest possible score being 100. The "G7 Democratic Countries Average" and "117 Sovereign States Average" were calculated based on the 2019 OBS dataset (International Budget Partnership, 2020))

government is subject to much more stringent budget oversight practices than Macao, despite similar budget oversight institutions under the Basic Laws of the two SARs. Unsurprisingly, both Hong Kong and Macao lag considerably behind the G7 democratic countries, whose scores average 76.7. Such a large difference reflects the nature of Hong Kong and Macao's hybrid political regimes, where the powers of their legislatures and SAIs are constrained by their semi-democratic, executive-dominant governments.

Deconstructing the overall scores into "legislative oversight" (OBS Questions 107–117) and "SAI oversight" (OBS Questions 118–124) scores indicated similar empirical patterns, with Hong Kong consistently attaining higher scores than Macao throughout the post-handover period, particularly with regard to "legislative oversight"—Hong Kong averaged 29 and 27.8 on "legislative oversight" and "SAI oversight," respectively; Macao's corresponding average scores were much lower, at 9.4 and 22.3

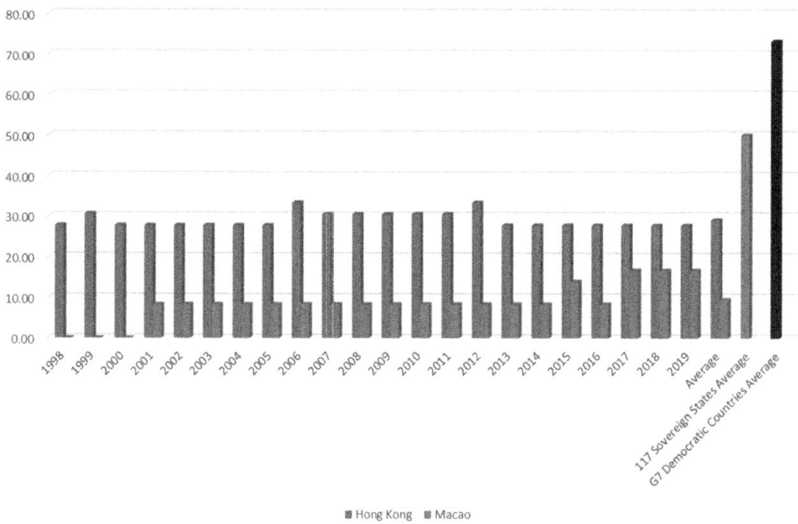

Fig. 5.2 Post-handover legislative oversight sub-scores of Hong Kong and Macao. (Note: Each fiscal year's score was quantified by averaging the scores attained by Hong Kong and Macao on Questions 107–117 (OBS questions on legislative oversight), the highest possible score being 100. The "G7 Democratic Countries Average" and "117 Sovereign States Average" were calculated based on the 2019 OBS dataset (International Budget Partnership, 2020))

(Figs. 5.2 and 5.3). This finding implies that Hong Kong's Legislative Council and Audit Commission are relatively more effective than Macao's Legislative Assembly and Commission of Audit in monitoring government budgets. However, when viewed in a global context, the legislatures and SAIs of both Hong Kong and Macao are considerably weaker than their G7 counterparts, which attained much higher average scores of 73.2 and 82.3 in the corresponding categories.

In Fig. 5.2, it is worth noting that Macao's scores of "composite budget oversight," "legislative oversight," and "SAI oversight" all substantially improved since handover of sovereignty in 1999 and in particular the "legislative oversight" sub-scores almost doubled since 2017. The overall improvement of budget oversight in Macao is related to the gradual enhancement of the oversight role of the Macao Legislative Assembly

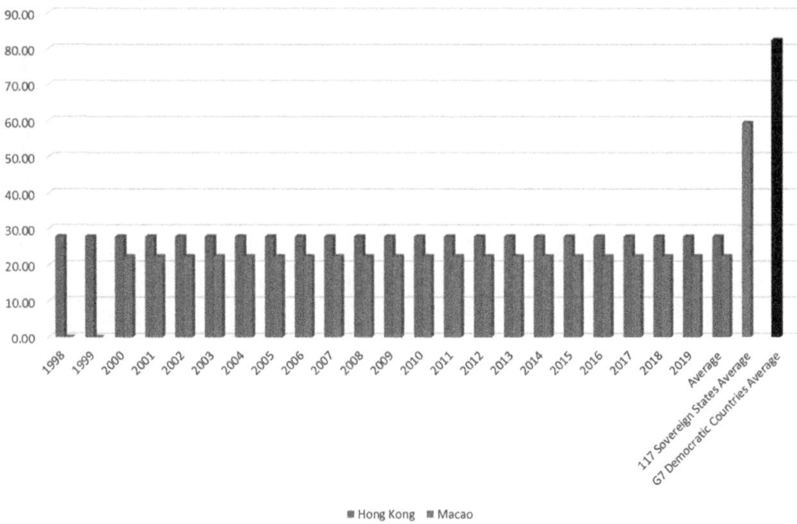

Fig. 5.3 Post-handover SAI oversight sub-scores for Hong Kong and Macao. (Note: Each fiscal year's score was quantified by averaging the scores attained by Hong Kong and Macao on Questions 118–124 (OBS questions on SAI oversight), the highest possible score being 100. The "G7 Democratic Countries Average" and "117 Sovereign States Average" were calculated based on the 2019 OBS dataset (International Budget Partnership, 2020))

since the handover (Yu, 2011), while the increase in "legislative oversight" since 2017 sub-scores is especially attributable to the legislative oversight reforms introduced in the aftermath of the corruption scandals associated with the Secretary for Transport and Public Works, Ao Man-long (Zheng & Wan, 2014: 146). Ao had been arrested by the Macau Commission Against Corruption in 2006 and was subsequently convicted on several charges of bribe-taking, abuse of power, and money laundering.[6] This corruption case led to a widespread demand within the Macao society for a more transparent public budgeting process (Zheng & Wan, 2014: 147), subsequently leading to the establishment of a new standing committee, the Follow-up Committee for Public Finance Affairs, in the Legislative

[6] For an account of the corruption case of Ao Man-long, see Lo (2020: 70–75).

Assembly in 2013,[7] and the enactment of the *Framework Law of Budget* in 2017.[8] Such institutional reforms had contributed to marked improvement in the oversight role of Macao's Legislative Assembly. Notwithstanding such improvements, Macao's "legislative oversight" scores remained significantly lower than that of Hong Kong.

Discussion: Why and How the Base of Opposition Politics Matters

Why did the Hong Kong and Macao governments experience different degrees of legislative and SAI monitoring despite having seemingly similar budget oversight institutions under the OCTS model? The most plausible explanation for this is the base of opposition politics—government budgets in Hong Kong are subject to much more stringent budget oversight practices than in Macao, owing to the fact that the former's budget oversight institutions are subject to a stronger scrutiny of opposition politics than the latter. In other words, the varying practices of budget oversight of Hong Kong and Macao are the consequences of their different bases of opposition politics. For empirical analysis, in this study the bases of opposition politics in Hong Kong and Macao are observed in three dimensions, namely, the democratic opposition, the media, and the civil society.

Democratic opposition: Since the introduction of direct elections to the legislature in 1991, Hong Kong's pro-democracy camp has continuously maintained a greater popular support base compared with the pro-regime camp, giving it an edge in geographical constituency elections (Ma, 2012). Despite Macao's earlier introduction of direct election to the legislature in 1976, its pro-democracy camp is relatively weaker in terms of resources, networks, and organization, making it too vulnerable to compete with the pro-regime camp in the electoral arena (Chan & Cheng, 2020; Zheng & Wan, 2014: 131). Consequently, since the handover, Hong Kong democrats have consistently occupied one-third of legislative seats, while their counterparts in Macao are numerically much smaller and

[7] For the official descriptions of the Follow-up Committee for Public Finance Affairs, see: https://www.al.gov.mo/zh/public-finances (Chinese only).

[8] The Framework Law of Budget provides more stringent regulations for the budgeting activities of the Macao government, such as imposing restrictions on virement of designated funds, strengthening the role of the Legislative Assembly over the monitoring of public works projects, and mandating the mid-term budget execution report submission to the Legislative Assembly. For the full text of the Framework Law of Budget, see: https://bo.io.gov.mo/bo/i/2017/35/lei15_cn.asp (Chinese and Portuguese only).

Table 5.3 Partisan distribution of Hong Kong's Legislative Council and Macao's Legislative Assembly

Year	*Pro-regime camp*		*Pro-democracy camp*		*Total*	
	N	*%*	*N*	*%*	*N*	*%*
Hong Kong						
2000	40	66.7	20	33.3	60	100
2004	35	58.3	25	41.7	60	100
2008	37	61.7	23	38.3	60	100
2012	43	61.4	27	38.6	70	100
2016	40	57.1	30	42.9	70	100
Macao						
2001	25	92.6	2	7.4	27	100
2005	26	89.7	3	10.3	29	100
2009	25	86.2	4	13.8	29	100
2013	29	87.9	4	12.1	33	100
2017	28	84.8	5	15.2	33	100

Source: Adapted from Ma (2020) for Hong Kong and Lo (2020: 128) for Macao

have generally secured fewer than one-fifth of the legislative seats (Table 5.3).[9]

With a relatively stronger minority position, Hong Kong's pro-democracy camp can make better use of legislative rules to pressurize the HKSAR government's budgetary proceedings through filibustering, raising questions, and proposing amendments. Hence, the pro-regime camp must always be fully mobilized to counter their scrutiny, which makes their budget oversight practices more stringent (Ma, 2012). In the 2019–2020 budget bill deliberations, for example, the Hong Kong democrats proposed a total of 156 bill amendments and 7109 written

[9] It is worth noting that the strong democratic opposition in Hong Kong than Macao is in turn a result of the higher degree of democratization of Hong Kong Legislative Council than the Macao Legislative Assembly. According to the empirical analysis of Fong (2019), the percentage of seats chosen by popular elections in the Hong Kong Legislative Council was increased from 31% in 1991–1995 to the 57.14% since 2016; while that of the Macao Assembly largely remained at the level of 35% to 42.42% from 1975 to present. The higher level of democratization of Hong Kong's legislature had certainly provided its democratic opposition a relatively greater room to thrive than their counterparts in Macao. For details, see Fong (2019).

questions.[10] Also, on many occasions, the pro-regime camp is as vocal as their pro-democracy counterparts in scrutinizing government budgets, particularly during successive years of budget surplus (Fong, 2019). Conversely, Macao's pro-democracy camp is constrained by its numerical disadvantage compared with the pro-regime camp and is therefore unable to strongly challenge the Macao government (Lo, 2020: 127). Macao's 2019 budget bill, thus, was easily passed unanimously by all legislators, including the democrats.[11] Therefore, it is not unexpected that the average time taken to pass government budgets in Hong Kong is much longer than that in Macao (Fig. 5.4); the Finance Committee of the Hong Kong Legislative Council is also more active than the Follow-up Committee for Public Finance Affairs of Macao's Legislative Assembly in terms of the meetings convened (Fig. 5.5).

Media: Despite the gradual erosion of press freedom after the handover, Hong Kong's media is still far more active than their Macao counterparts in terms of monitoring the government. The stronger watchdog role of Hong Kong's media is not simply attributable to its larger scale (Table 5.4), but also the more assertive media culture and environment. Notwithstanding the growing pressures of self-censorship in Hong Kong, surveys of professional journalists revealed that most of them saw monitoring the government as an important media function and that the liberal democratic ideal remains the foundation of journalism (Chan & Lee, 2012). Macao's media firms are relatively more structurally dependent on the political establishment for annual government subsidies to sustain their operations. Thus, the media culture in Macao tends to be more compliant with a lack of investigative reporting on government performance (Lo, 2020: 70). Except for a few pro-democracy Internet news media such as Macau Concealers and All About Macau, all mainstream media firms in Macao are pro-regime and rarely feature negative reports on the political establishment (Lo, 2020: 113; Zheng & Wan, 2014: 147).

Given the aforementioned context, government's budgets and audit reports are more extensively covered by the Hong Kong media compared to the Macao media (Figs. 5.6 and 5.7), with pro-regime media, such as

[10] For the record of budget amendments proposed by Hong Kong's democrats on 2019–2020 budget, see: https://www.legco.gov.hk/yr18-19/english/pre_rul/pre20190506-ref-e.pdf; for the record of written questions raised by them, see: https://www.legco.gov.hk/yr18-19/english/fc/fc/minutes/sfc_rpt.pdf.

[11] For the record of deliberation of Macao's 2019 budget bill, see: https://www.al.gov.mo/zh/law/2018/358 (Chinese and Portuguese only).

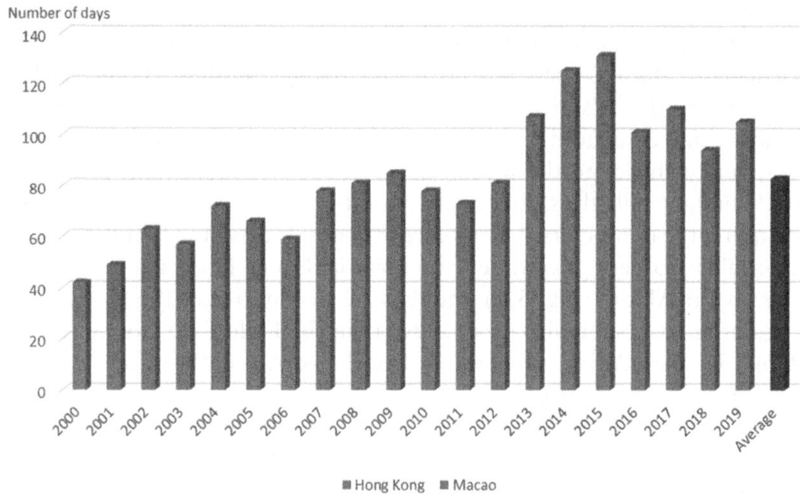

Fig. 5.4 Time required for passage of government budgets in Hong Kong's Legislative Council and Macao's Legislative Assembly. (Source: Author's own analysis based on the available information from the official websites of Hong Kong's Legislative Council (https://www.legco.gov.hk/database_leg_pro/chinese/bills/bills.htm) and Macao's Legislative Assembly (https://www.al.gov.mo/zh/law). Note: The Y-axis denotes the number of calendar days required for the passage of the budget bills in the respective fiscal years, calculated by deducting the third reading dates from the first reading dates)

the *Oriental Daily*, in Hong Kong usually joining pro-democracy media, such as the *Apple Daily*, in critically appraising the government's budgetary activities. For example, on the release of the Audit Commission's value-for-money reports on 17 April 2019, all local newspapers, ranging from pro-democracy to pro-regime, had negative headlines in the following days, criticizing the mismanagement of resources by several government departments such as the Transport, Civil Aid Service, and Labour Departments.[12]

[12] According to WiseNews Search Engine, there were a total of 71 Chinese news reports on 18 April 2019, the date following the release of the value-for-money reports by the Audit Commission. For full text of the audit reports, see: https://www.aud.gov.hk/eng/pubpr_arpt/rpt_72.htm.

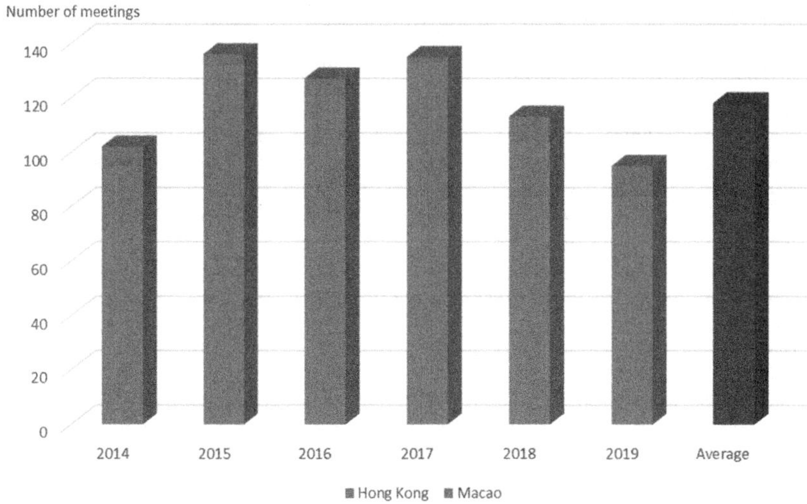

Fig. 5.5 Number of meetings held by the Finance Committee of Hong Kong's Legislative Council and Follow-up Committee for Public Finance Affairs of Macao's Legislative Assembly. (Source: Author's own analysis based on available information from the official websites of Hong Kong's Legislative Council (https://www.legco.gov.hk/general/english/fc/fc1620.htm) and Macao's Legislative Assembly (https://www.al.gov.mo/zh/public-finances). Note: For Hong Kong, the Y-axis denotes the total number of meetings of the entire Finance Committee, the Establishment Subcommittee, and the Public Works Subcommittee)

Civil society: Hong Kong's civil society organizations are more active than their counterparts in Macao in challenging government policies, including those related to public budgeting. Since its coming of age in the 1970s, Hong Kong's civil society has developed a culture of pressurizing the government through protests, petitions, and signature campaigns (Chan, 2012). Contrarily, government–society relations in Macao are more harmonious, owing to a different power balance between pro-regime and independent civil society groups. On the one hand, there are several powerful, broad-based, pro-regime groups that readily mobilize popular support for the Macao government, such as the Macao Chamber of Commerce, Macao Federation of Trade Unions, General Union of Neighbourhood Associations, and Women's General Association, as well as the recently founded Jiangmen Communal Society, Fujian Association,

Table 5.4 Mass media in Hong Kong and Macao

	2012	*2013*	*2014*	*2015*	*2016*	*2017*	*2018*	*2019*
Hong Kong								
Newspapers in Chinese	25	28	29	26	28	37	50	53
Newspapers in English and other languages	26	27	27	27	26	31	30	29
Television and radio stations	27	29	29	28	26	23	22	20
Macao								
Newspapers in Chinese	10	10	11	11	13	13	13	13
Newspapers in Portuguese and other languages	6	6	6	6	6	6	5	5
Television and radio stations	10	10	10	9	10	11	11	9

Source: Author's own analysis based on the information available on the official website of the Hong Kong Yearbook (https://www.yearbook.gov.hk) and Macao Yearbook of Statistics (https://www.dsec.gov.mo/en-US/Home/Publication/YearbookOfStatistics)

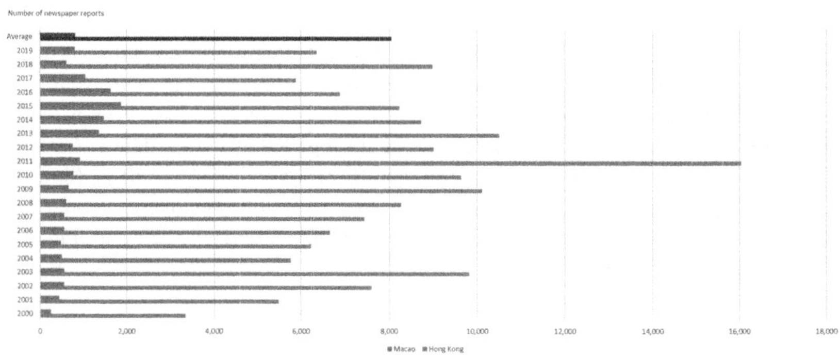

Fig. 5.6 Number of news reports on the government budgets of Hong Kong and Macao. (Source: Data retrieved from the WiseNews Search Engine, using the keyword "budget" (in Chinese))

and Federation of Zhuhai Society. On the other hand, a stronger apolitical culture and smaller middle-professional class in Macao effectively leave limited room for developing independent civil society groups (Lo, 2020: 128–129, 266–267; Ping, 2011).

Given the different trajectories of a "vibrant civil society" in Hong Kong and "suppressed civil society" in Macao (Chan & Cheng, 2020), the former's government budgets are subject to a higher degree of scrutiny from civil society than the latter's, as demonstrated by the disparate numbers of budget protests in the two SARs (Fig. 5.8).

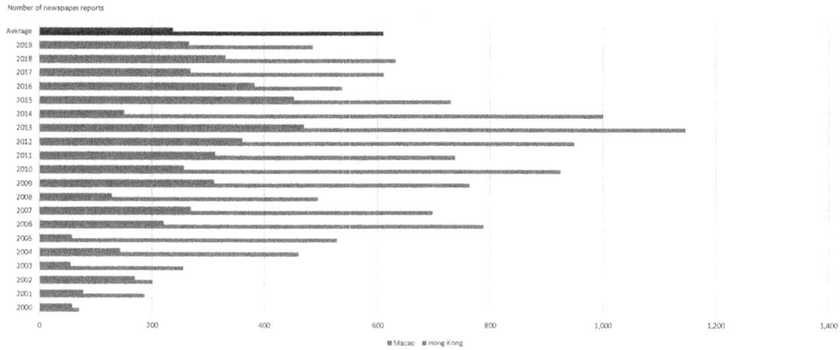

Fig. 5.7 Number of news reports on the audit reports of Hong Kong and Macao. (Source: Data retrieved from the WiseNews Search Engine, using the keyword "audit report" (in Chinese))

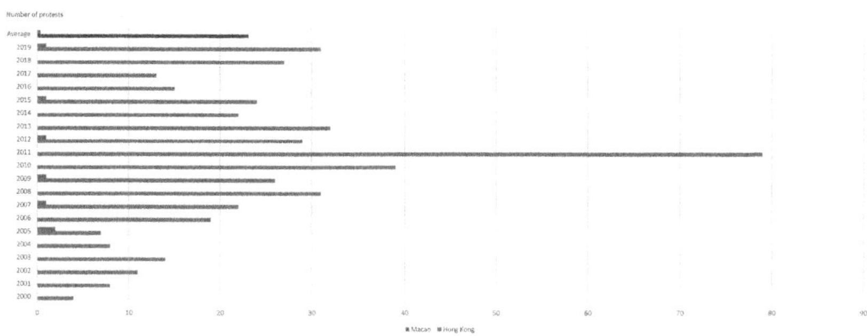

Fig. 5.8 Number of budget protests in Hong Kong and Macao. (Source: Author's own analysis based on data retrieved from the WiseNews Search Engine, using the keyword "budget" (in Chinese) to search all budget-related news reports, followed by manual coding of protest events if related to government budgets. Protest events reported by different newspapers were counted only once)

To summarize, the stronger base of opposition politics in Hong Kong helps sustain the modus operandi of its legislative and SAI oversight institutions and explains why Hong Kong and Macao are subject to different budget oversight practices, despite having similar prima facie budget oversight institutions under the OCTS model.

However, it must be noted that Hong Kong's relatively stronger base of opposition politics does not fundamentally alter the constitutional constraints imposed by the Basic Law on its legislative and SAI oversights. Notwithstanding their stronger influence, Hong Kong's pro-democracy camp, civil society, and media remain incompetent to create a real policy impact on government budgets when faced with an executive-dominant government, a pro-regime majority, and procedural constraints on legislators. In other words, the difference in budget oversight practices between Hong Kong and Macao is a matter of *degree*, but not of *kind*.

Conclusions

This chapter is a pioneering attempt to study budget oversight at the territorial autonomy level. Applying the OBS methodology, this comparative case study of Hong Kong and Macao goes beyond the mainstream public budgeting literature by reorienting the research focus from sovereign states to territorial autonomies. Limited by its nature as binary case studies, the findings of this chapter—on how the base of opposition politics has affected budget oversight practices—cannot be straightforwardly generalized to other territorial autonomies. Still, this chapter successfully applies the comparative tools of the OBS to the context of territorial autonomies, highlighting how budget oversight of Hong Kong and Macao has been structured by their semi-democratic regimes and laying the foundation for future expansion of such frameworks to a larger number of cases.

Generally speaking, when compared with territorial autonomies worldwide, Hong Kong and Macao have been privileged with full fiscal autonomous powers (e.g. deciding on their own budgets, maintaining their own separate taxation systems, and keeping all budgetary resources for their own use), while other territorial autonomies as documented by scholars thus far such as Åland, Catalonia, and Scotland are operated under different degrees of central control (e.g. intra-state transfer system and state-wide taxation regimes). Yet, other territorial autonomies normally have a higher degree of democratization than both Hong Kong and Macao (see Ghai & Woodman, 2013). Whether and how the budget oversight of territorial autonomies worldwide are structured by their different parameters of fiscal autonomy and varying degrees of democratization are certainly theoretically and practically significant topics for future comparative budgeting studies.

Since the 2000s, critics within the social science community have challenged state-centrism and the "methodological nationalism" that entails the adoption of the sovereign state as the default unit of analysis (Wimmer & Glick Schiller, 2002). Political scientists from the fields of comparative politics and international relations have also queried the state-centric approach (Orenstein & Schmitz, 2006) and made attempts to study multi-level territorial politics across sub-state, state, and supra-state jurisdictions (Hepburn & Detterbeck, 2018).

Thus far, this intellectual trend has not percolated to the field of comparative budgeting, with studies on sub-state jurisdictions remaining secondary and those on territorial autonomies almost absent. Comparative political scholars have called for "methodological pluralism" (Giraud & Maggetti, 2015; Guiraudon, 2020); comparative budgeting scholars should also heed this call.

Further Readings

- International Budget Partnership. (2019). *Guide to the Open Budget Questionnaire: An Explanation of the Questions and the Response Options*. Washington, DC. Available At: https://www.internationalbudget.org/sites/default/files/2020-04/2019_Guide_and_Questionnaire_EN.pdf.

The latest version of OBS standard questionnaire, which provides an explanation of the 142 questions and the response options.

- International Budget Partnership. (2020). *Open Budget Survey 2019*. Washington, DC. Available At: https://www.internationalbudget.org/open-budget-survey/open-budget-survey-2019.

The latest, seventh OBS report, which assessed and compared the state of budgetary openness, public participation, and oversight in 117 countries.

- Warner, R. (2018). *Making the Most of the Budget Cycle: The Budget Oversight Stage*. In: International Budget Partnership: Open Budgets Blog. Available At: https://www.internationalbudget.org/2018/04/making-budget-cycle-budget-oversight-stage.

An overview of the measurement of budget oversight according to the OBS methodologies.

Bibliography

Chan, E. Y. M. (2012). Civil Society. In W. M. Lam, P. L. T. Lui, & W. Wilson (Eds.), *Contemporary Hong Kong Government and Politics* (pp. 179–198). Hong Kong University Press.

Chan, J. M., & Lee, F. L. F. (2012). Mass Media and Public Opinion. In W. M. Lam, P. L. T. Lui, & W. Wilson (Eds.), *Contemporary Hong Kong Government and Politics* (pp. 233–246). Hong Kong University Press.

Chan, W. Y., & Cheng, E. W. (2020). State-Society Relations in Hong Kong and Macau: A Historical Institutionalist Analysis. In M. U. Ieong (Ed.), *Macau 20 Years After the Handover: Changes and Challenges Under "One Country, Two Systems"* (pp. 121–134). Routledge.

Chou, B. K. P. (2013). Elections in Hong Kong: International Perspectives and Implications for China. In P. E. Lam, Y. Qin, & M. Yang (Eds.), *China and East Asia: After the Wall Street Crisis* (Vol. 33, pp. 75–99). World Scientific Publishing.

De Renzio, P., & Masud, H. (2011). Measuring and Promoting Budget Transparency: The Open Budget Index as a Research and Advocacy Tool. *Governance, S1*, 607–616.

Fong, B. C. H. (2015). The Politics of Budget Surpluses: The Case of China's HKSAR. *International Review of Administrative Sciences, 81*(1), 134–157.

Fong, B. C. H. (2018). Executive-Legislative Disconnection in the HKSAR: The Erosion of the Legislative Support Base of the Chief Executives, 1997–2017. In B. C. H. Fong & T. L. Lui (Eds.), *Hong Kong: 20 Years After the Handover – Emerging Social and Institutional Fractures After 1997* (pp. 45–71). Palgrave Macmillan.

Fong, B. C. H. (2019). Democratization and Budget Openness: Evidences from Hong Kong, Macao, and Taiwan. *International Review of Administrative Sciences.* Article First Published Online: 8 July 2019. https://doi.org/10.1177/0020852319845453

Ghai, Y. P., & Woodman, S. (2013). *Practising Self-Government: A Comparative Study of Autonomous Regions.* Cambridge University Press.

Giraud, O., & Maggetti, M. (2015). Methodological Pluralism. In D. Braun & M. Maggetti (Eds.), *Comparative Politics: Theoretical and Methodological Challenges* (pp. 90–124). Edward Elgar.

Guiraudon, V. (2020). Methodological Pluralism in European Political Science. In B. Thibaud, I. Engeli, & D. Garzia (Eds.), *Political Science in Europe. Achievements, Challenges, Prospects* (pp. 63–82). ECPR Press.

Hague, R., & Harrop, M. (2013). *Comparative Government and Politics: An Introduction.* Palgrave Macmillan.

Heald, D. (2012). Why is Transparency About Public Expenditure so Elusive? *International Review of Administrative Sciences, 78*(1), 30–49.

Hepburn, E., & Detterbeck, K. (2018). Introduction to the Handbook of Territorial Politics. In E. Hepburn & K. Detterbeck (Eds.), *Handbook of Territorial Politics* (pp. 1–14). Edward Elgar.

International Budget Partnership. (2019). *Guide to the Open Budget Questionnaire: An Explanation of the Questions and the Response Options.* Washington, DC. Retrieved February 3, 2021, from https://www.internationalbudget.org/sites/default/files/2020-04/2019_Guide_and_Questionnaire_EN.pdf

International Budget Partnership. (2020). *Open Budget Survey 2019.* Washington, DC. Retrieved February 3, 2021, from https://www.internationalbudget.org/open-budget-survey/open-budget-survey-2019

International Budget Partnership. (2021). *About.* Washington, DC. Retrieved February 3, 2021, from https://www.internationalbudget.org/open–budget–survey/about

International Monetary Fund. (2020). *How the IMF is Promoting Transparent and Accountable Use of COVID–19 Financial Assistance.* Washington, DC. Retrieved February 3, 2021, from https://www.imf.org/en/about/factsheets/sheets/2020/04/30/how–imf–covid19–financial–help–is–used

Lo, S. S. H. (2020). *Casino Capitalism, Society and Politics in China's Macau.* Cambridge Scholars Publishing.

Ma, N. (2012). Political Parties and Elections. In W. M. Lam, P. L. T. Lui, & W. Wong (Eds.), *Contemporary Hong Kong Government and Politics* (pp. 159–177). Hong Kong University Press.

Ma, N. (2020). China's Influence on Hong Kong's Elections: Evidence from Legislative Council Elections. In B. C. H. Fong, J. M. Wu, & A. J. Nathan (Eds.), *China's Influence and the Center-Periphery Tug of War in Hong Kong, Taiwan and Indo-Pacific* (pp. 91–104). Routledge.

Orenstein, M. A., & Schmitz, H. P. (2006). The New Transnationalism and Comparative Politics. *Comparative Politics, 38*(4), 479–500.

Organization for Economic Co-Operation and Development. (2020). *Legislative Budget Oversight of Emergency Responses: Experiences During the Coronavirus (COVID 19) Pandemic.* Paris. Retrieved February 3, 2021, from https://www.oecd.org/coronavirus/policy–responses/legislative–budget–oversight–of–emergency–responses–experiences–during–the–coronavirus–covid–19–pandemic–ba4f2ab5

Peters, B. G. (2013). *Strategies for Comparative Research in Political Science.* Palgrave Macmillan.

Ping, A. L. S. (2011). Challenges and Threats to Traditional Associations. In N. M. Lam & I. Scott (Eds.), *Gaming, Governance and Public Policy in Macao* (pp. 75–88). Hong Kong University Press.

Santiso, C. (2009). *The Political Economy of Government Auditing: Financial Governance and the Rule of Law in Latin America and Beyond.* Routledge.

Seifert, J., Carlitz, R., & Mondo, E. (2013). The Open Budget Index (OBS) as a Comparative Statistical Tool. *Journal of Comparative Policy Analysis: Research and Practice, 15*(1), 87–101.

United Nations for Human Rights Office of the High Commissioner. (2017). *Realizing Human Rights Through Government Budgets.* New York: United Nations.

Warner, R. (2018). *Making the Most of the Budget Cycle: The Budget Oversight Stage.* International Budget Partnership: Open Budgets Blog. Retrieved February 3, 2021, from https://www.internationalbudget.org/2018/04/making-budget-cycle-budget-oversight-stage

Wehner, J. (2006). Assessing the Power of the Purse: An Index of Legislative Budget Institutions. *Political Studies, 54*(4), 767–785.

Wimmer, A., & Glick Schiller, N. (2002). Methodological Nationalism and Beyond: Nation-State Building, Migration and the Social Sciences. *Global Networks, 2*(4), 301–334.

Yu, E. W. Y. (2011). Executive-Legislature Relationships and the Development of Public Policy. In L. Newman & I. Scott (Eds.), *Gaming, Governance and Public Policy in Macao* (pp. 57–64). Hong Kong University Press.

Zheng, V., & Wan, P. S. (2014). *Gambling Dynamism: The Macao Miracle.* Springer.

CHAPTER 6

Budget Allocation

This chapter examines the dynamics of deficit politics and surplus politics through a comparative analysis of Hong Kong and Singapore.

While most countries are facing budget deficits, some countries and regions are experiencing budget surpluses. However, surplus politics, and its comparison with deficit politics, remains underexplored. In the comparative budgeting literature, existing research focuses overwhelmingly on deficit politics. Scholars and researchers have placed great emphasis on examining the deficit politics that Western democracies have confronted because of their consecutive years of budget deficits, and they have almost lost sight of the surplus politics that some other countries and regions have encountered due to their consecutive years of budget surpluses. Yet, what are the similarities and differences between deficit politics and surplus politics?

This chapter intends to address this underexplored research question through an exploratory comparative study of Hong Kong and Singapore. As far as comparative budgeting studies are concerned, surplus politics is

Originally published in a slightly different form under the title of "Deficit Politics and Surplus Politics: A Comparative Study of Hong Kong and Singapore," reprinted from *International Public Management Journal*, Article first published online: 1 April 2021, https://doi.org/10.1080/10967494.2021.1903633, by permission of Taylor & Francis.

B. C. H. Fong, *Hong Kong Public Budgeting*, Hong Kong Studies Reader Series, https://doi.org/10.1007/978-981-16-5363-6_6

an under-studied phenomenon awaiting further exploration, and studying the dynamics of surplus politics and comparing it with deficit politics can help establish a full understanding of budgetary politics. Therefore, this chapter is a pioneer attempt to investigate the dynamics of both deficit politics and surplus politics through an exploratory comparative study of Hong Kong and Singapore. It fills the theoretical and empirical gap in the comparative budgeting literature by broadening the research focus from deficit politics to surplus politics and providing a comparative framework to study the dynamics of both red-ink years and black-ink years.

Research Context

In the 1980s, when Wildavsky (1986: 7) classically defined that in every government budget lies conflicts, he did not specify whether budgetary conflicts will be similar or different between deficit years and surplus years. In the decades to come when comparative budgeting studies grow and expand tremendously, deficit politics as budgetary conflicts arising from the balancing of deficits (Rubin, 2020: 197–242) has been the focus of budgetary scholars. There is a large volume of literature on deficit politics with the focus placed on a particular democracy such as the United States (e.g. Kettl, 2003; Morgan, 2009) or a selected number of democracies from a comparative perspective (e.g. Ide & Park, 2015; Imbeau & Pétry, 2004; Posner, 2013). In the conception of many comparative budgeting scholars, deficits and public debts have been assumed as the dominant phenomenon worldwide, particularly in the aftermaths of the 2008 Financial Crisis in the United States and the 2009 Euro Sovereign Debt Crisis (see Guess & LeLoup, 2021: 8–10).

However, does deficit politics provide the full picture of budgetary politics? According to the global database once maintained by the World Bank in the 2000s,[1] within the eight-year time period between 2002 and 2009, 65 countries and regions (67%) faced cash deficits for all or most of the recorded years; 23 countries and regions (23.7%) achieved cash surpluses for all or most of the recorded years; and 9 countries and regions (9.3%) experienced an equal number of deficit years and surplus years. The 23 countries and regions that experienced consistent budget surpluses

[1] The World Bank Data. Public Sector—Cash Surplus/Deficit (% of GDP). https://databank.worldbank.org/metadataglossary/wdi-database-archives-(beta)/series/GC.BAL.CASH.GD.ZS. Accessed 6 September 2016.

have a variety of political, socio-economic, and cultural backgrounds, namely Algeria, Angola, Australia, Bulgaria, Bahrain, Canada, Chile, Congo, Denmark, Estonia, Finland, Hong Kong, Iran, Korea, Macao, Norway, New Zealand, Oman, Russia, Singapore, Seychelles, Thailand, and Trinidad and Tobago.

The fact that dozens of countries and regions have experienced consecutive years of budget surpluses gives rise to an important, so far under-explored, research question: what are the similarities and differences between deficit politics and surplus politics? In his later publication *The New Politics of the Budgetary Process* in the 2000s, Wildavsky (2004) finally made the first attempt to explore surplus politics with reference to the massive budget surpluses accumulated in the final years of Bill Clinton's presidency in the United States. Wildavsky observed that surplus politics is "no less difficult than" deficit politics, as the White House and Republican-controlled Congress contended with each other over the allocation of surpluses—the Republicans wanted to cut taxes and increase defence spending, while the White House preferred to use the surpluses to pay off debt (Wildavsky, 2004: 208–212). Surplus politics continued in the first year of George W. Bush's presidency when he proposed a historical tax cut of USD 1.6 trillion, an expansion of the defence budget, and to freeze domestic discretionary spending. The president's proposals were met with strong opposition in the evenly divided Senate, with the Democrats requesting a smaller tax cut and an increase in domestic discretionary spending (Wildavsky, 2004: 212–214).

If both deficit and surplus give rise to budget battles, as pointed out by Wildavsky with reference to the case of the United States in the late 1990s, then what are the similarities and differences between deficit politics and surplus politics? This chapter explores this important, but under-investigated, research question empirically through a comparative study of Hong Kong and Singapore.

Research Case Background

Most-Similar-System Comparison of Hong Kong and Singapore

There are two major reasons for selecting Hong Kong and Singapore as binary cases. First, because Hong Kong and Singapore overlap on many important aspects such as historical background (former British colonies), administrative legacies (British-style civil service and public finance systems), legal systems (common law systems), socio-economic structures (global cities), population (Chinese migrant society), and culture (Chinese cultural orientation). Therefore, they are ideal candidates for implementing a 'most-similar-system' research design strategy (Hague & Harrop, 2013: 368; Peters, 2013: 39–44).

Second, both Hong Kong and Singapore have faced consistent budget surpluses in the recent ten-year span after experiencing a few years of budget deficits in the early 2000s (Figs. 6.1 and 6.2). Therefore, comparing Hong Kong and Singapore will allow us to trace the budgetary politics that they have experienced in their recent cycles of deficits and surpluses, facilitating both vertical (i.e. comparing Hong Kong from deficit years to surplus years, and Singapore from deficit years to surplus years) and horizontal comparison (i.e. comparing the deficit years of Hong Kong and Singapore, and then their surplus years).

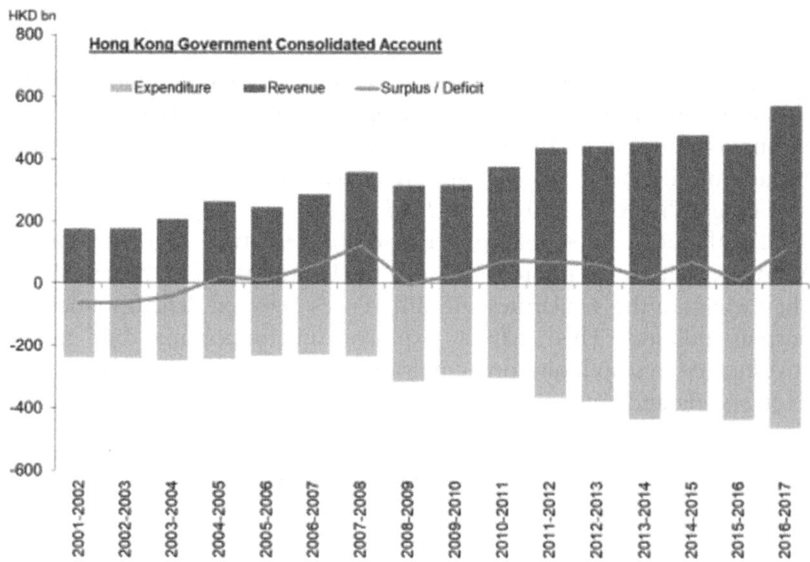

Fig. 6.1 Hong Kong government's consolidated account (2001/02–2016/17). (Source: Author's own research based on the statistical tables available at the Hong Kong government Census and Statistics Department's website at http://www.censtatd.gov.hk)

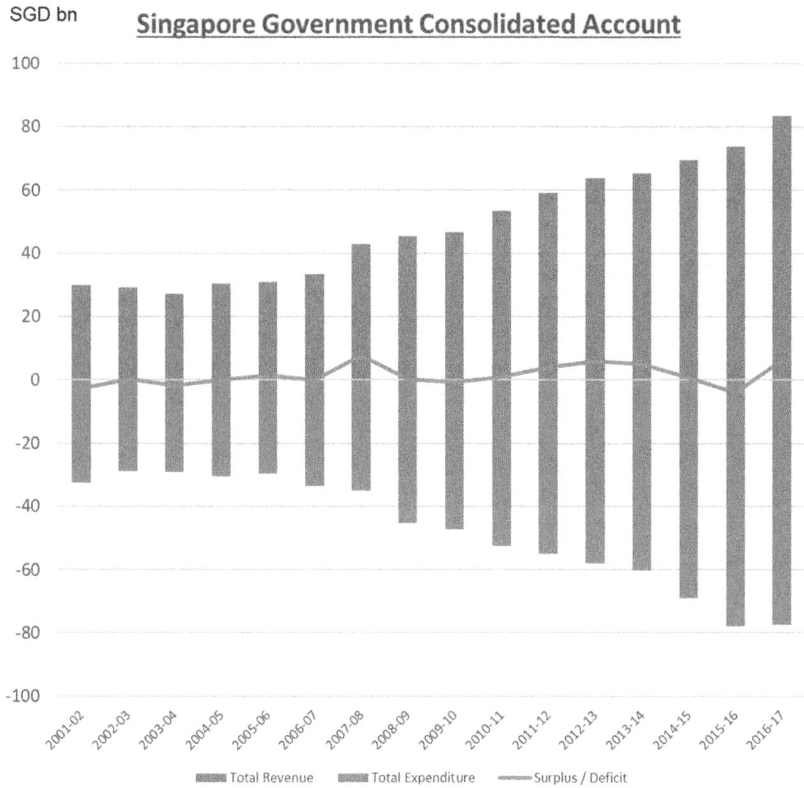

Fig. 6.2 Singapore government's consolidated account (2001/02–2016/17). (Source: Author's own research based on the statistical tables available at the Singapore Government Ministry of Finance's website at http://www.singapore-budget.gov.sg)

It is worth nothing that the unit of analysis of this comparative study is "primary government" within public budgeting literature, which is defined as "a state or local government that has a separately elected governing body and is fiscally independent of other state or local governments" (Wang, 2014: 122). Constitutionally speaking, Hong Kong is a territorial autonomy of China with the official name of Hong Kong Special Administrative Region (HKSAR). Yet, as far as public finance is concerned,

Hong Kong is a "primary government," which is essentially on par with Singapore.

The Public Budgeting Systems of Hong Kong and Singapore

Sharing a common historical legacy as former crown colonies of the British Empire, both Hong Kong and Singapore have inherited their public budgeting systems from the British colonial master and the legacies of fiscal conservatism (Cheung, 2006). Interestingly, the British colonial-style public budgeting system has remained largely intact in both modern Hong Kong and Singapore and was constitutionalized as part of their post-colonial political systems, notwithstanding that the two city-states have followed different political trajectories after the departure of the colonialists.

Hong Kong's public budgeting system[2] is one of the many British heritages developed during colonial rule (1841–1997) and was preserved under Chinese rule (1997–). Generally speaking, fiscal conservatism is the hallmark of Hong Kong's public finance system, which was a by-product of the British colonialists' strategy to "run the Empire on the cheap" (Brendon, 2007: 334). Because the British had imposed a stringent fiscal discipline across all its colonies, since the founding of the colony in 1841, the Hong Kong government had adopted financial prudence as the foundation of its budgetary system all along (Scott, 2010: 152; Fong, 2015, 2019). As a consequence of the dismantling of the British Empire in the post-Second World War period, Hong Kong had undergone a process of "informal devolution" with extensive autonomous powers devolved from London to Hong Kong, including the powers to fully decide its own annual budgets in 1958 and to manage its foreign exchange reserves in 1972 (Goodstadt, 2009: 49–70; Fong, 2020). Such full-fledged fiscal autonomy, together with the rules of financial prudence, was codified by virtue of Article 5 of Annex I of the 1984 Sino-British Joint Declaration,[3] and Articles 106 to 108 of the 1990 Hong Kong Special Administrative

[2] For an overview of Hong Kong's public finance system, see Cheung (2005) and Fong (2015).

[3] Article V of Annex I of the Sino-British Joint Declaration stipulated that "The Hong Kong Special Administrative Region shall deal on its own with financial matters, including disposing of its financial resources and drawing up its budgets and its final accounts." For full text of the Sino-British Joint Declaration, see: http://www.cmab.gov.hk/en/issues/joint.htm.

Region Basic Law.[4] Their provisions stipulate that after the transfer of sovereignty in 1997, Hong Kong shall continue to fully decide its own budgetary matters according to prudent fiscal disciplines.

As another former British crown colony, Singapore's public finance system[5] had developed a similar historical legacy of fiscal conservativism featuring financial self-support and balanced budgets under colonial rule (Sugimoto & Tan, 2011). Such prudent fiscal discipline had been subsequently institutionalized into the Singapore Constitution after Independence in 1965,[6] with three important fiscal rules incorporated: restricting the current government from using the reserves accumulated by the previous terms of government, barring the current government from using more than 50% of the net investment returns earned from past reserves to fund its expenditures, and empowering both parliament and the president as fiscal guardians to approve the use of reserves under the so-called two-key safety mechanism by virtue of Article 147(4a), Article 142(3), and Article 144(2), respectively (Blöndal, 2006). Therefore, despite its transformation from a crown colony to a dominion and later to a sovereign state throughout the twentieth century, the Singapore government had followed prudent financial management practices all along. Because of this, Singapore had largely maintained fiscal balance in the pre-Second World War period and had successfully maintained substantial budget surpluses for most of the years between the 1950s and the 1990s (Sugimoto & Tan, 2011). Research has indicated that Singapore's prudent financial management (and the resultant capital accumulation) was a major pillar of its successful "developmental state" model (Asher et al., 2015).

Research Design

This chapter empirically examines the dynamics of budgetary politics confronting Hong Kong and Singapore in their recent cycles of deficits and surpluses from 2001–2002 to 2016–2017 according to the following three-step research design. The first part concerns the measurement of budgetary demand. For this purpose, the theoretical concept of "media

[4] For full text of the Articles 106 to 108 of the Basic Law, see: http://www.basiclaw.gov.hk.

[5] For an overview of Singapore's public finance system, see Asher (1989).

[6] For full text of Article 147(4a), Article 142(3), and Article 144(2) of the Singaporean constitution, see: https://sso.agc.gov.sg/Act/CONS1963.

content analysis" from policy science literature was adopted. According to Oehl et al. (2016), public opinion surveys, as indicators of "policy demand," have many issues such as high costs, limited commensurability of data across different countries and regions, failure to provide consistent time series data, impossibility to fill the data gaps ex post, and so on. Therefore, Oehl et al. (2016) developed a novel research framework known as "media content analysis" to observe "policy demands." Accordingly, the viewpoints of non-governmental actors expressed in the form of news interviews, reports, and commentaries can serve as a meaningful proxy for "policy demands." Oehl et al. (2016) proposed to observe policy demands through three measurable indicators:

- *Media salience*: The number of articles on a particular policy demand relative to the total number of articles published in the respective newspapers within a given time (i.e. salience aspect of a policy demand). The higher the number, the more salient the policy demand.
- *Politicization of public debate*: The degree of politicization of a particular policy demand within the media, defined as the total number of claims divided by the total number of articles published in the respective newspapers within a given time (i.e. debate intensity of a policy demand). The higher the number, the more contested the public debate on the subject.
- *Published opinion*: The ratio of positive and negative claims for a particular policy demand expressed by non-governmental actors in the respective newspapers within a given time, defined as positive claims minus negative claims divided by the total number of claims (i.e. opinion aspect of a policy demand). The higher the positive number, the stronger the claims for the policy demand; the higher the negative number, the stronger the claims against the policy demand; and the closer the number to zero, the more even the distribution between the two claims.

Following this framework, the budgetary demand of non-governmental actors in Hong Kong and Singapore was traced through online news archives. "Non-governmental actors" are defined as any person or organization other than officials and executive council/cabinet members of the Hong Kong and Singapore governments. As the focus of this research is to examine the budgetary politics surrounding the annual government budgets of Hong Kong and Singapore, newspaper articles related to supplementary estimates were excluded from the analysis, including those about Finance Committee Proposals to be vetted by the Hong Kong Legislative Council and Supplementary Supply Bills to be examined by the Singapore Parliament. Based on these parameters, a total of 8070 and 3942 news articles were coded for Hong Kong and Singapore, respectively, from the 2001–2002 budget to the 2016–2017 budget. Such labour-intensive coding was completed by field researchers in two years' time.

All the media content that was initially collected was first grouped under headings corresponding to annual budgets according to the "prior 12-month rule." For example, media content in Hong Kong from April 2001 to March 2002 was placed under the 2002–2003 Budget Speech as announced on 6 March 2002, while media content in Singapore from June 2001 to May 2002 was placed under the 2002 Budget Statement, as announced on 6 May 2002. Then, the media content was categorized into six types of budgetary demand: "increasing tax," "reducing/freezing tax," "increasing expenditure," "reducing/freezing expenditure," "maintaining/increasing reserves," and "spending reserves." Finally, the media content was converted into indicators of "media salience," "published opinion," and "politicization of public debate" (Table 6.1).

The second part of the research concerned the measurement of budgetary output. For this purpose, the "estimated" total taxation revenue and total expenditure, as announced by the Hong Kong and Singapore governments in their corresponding annual budgets, were coded. Instead of using the "actual" figures to be announced one year after budget execution, the "estimated" figures were adopted because they are more direct indicators of the two governments' responsiveness to budgetary demand-making towards the corresponding annual budgets. As the Singapore government keeps its reserve confidential, only taxation and expenditure were covered when coding the budgetary output (Table 6.2).

The third part of the research studied the empirical pattern of budgetary demand (Table 6.3) and examined the correlation between budgetary demand and budgetary output (Table 6.4), with data compared both vertically within Hong Kong/Singapore itself and horizontally between the two places.

Table 6.1 Operationalization of the indicators of budgetary demand for Hong Kong and Singapore

	Tax	*Expenditure*	*Reserve*
Media salience	• "Number of tax-related news articles" relative to the "number of Budget Speech-related news articles published in the respective newspapers.	• "Number of expenditure-related news articles" relative to the "number of Budget Speech-related news articles published in the respective newspapers.	• "Number of reserve-related news articles" relative to the "number of Budget Speech-related news articles published in the respective newspapers.
Politicization of public debate	• Degree of politicization of tax issue = total sum of the "number of claims made by non-governmental actors in favour of offering tax breaks" (1) and the "number of claims made by non-governmental actors against offering tax breaks (including preservation of the status quo or more taxes)" (2) divided by the "number of tax-related news articles published in the respective newspapers."	• Degree of politicization of expenditure issue = total sum of the "number of claims made by non-governmental actors in favour of increasing expenditure" (3) and the "number of claims made by non-governmental actors against increasing expenditure (including preservation of the status quo or less expenditure)" (4) divided by the "number of expenditure-related news articles."	• Degree of politicization of reserve issue = total sum of the "number of claims made by non-governmental actors in favour of spending reserve" (5) and the "number of claims made by non-governmental actors against spending reserve (including preservation of the status quo or more reserve)" (6) divided by the "number of reserve-related news articles."

(*continued*)

Table 6.1 (continued)

	Tax	*Expenditure*	*Reserve*
Published opinion	• Ratio of positive and negative claims on tax issue = "number of claims made by non-governmental actors in favour of offering tax breaks" (1) minus the "number of claims made by non-governmental actors against offering tax breaks (including preservation of the status quo or more taxes)" (2) and then divided by the "total number of claims on tax."	• Ratio of positive and negative claims on expenditure issue = "number of claims made by non-governmental actors in favour of increasing expenditure" (3) minus the "number of claims made by non-governmental actors against increasing expenditure (including preservation of the status quo or less expenditure)" (4) and then divided by the "total number of claims on expenditure."	• Ratio of positive and negative claims on reserve issue = "number of claims made by non-governmental actors in favour of spending reserve" (5) minus the "number of claims made by non-governmental actors against spending reserve (including preservation of the status quo or more reserve)" (6) and then divided by the "total number of claims on reserve."

Notes: (1) The news articles coded for Hong Kong were obtained from the news archives of *Ming Pao* and the *South China Morning Post*, which were downloaded from the WiseNews platform by searching for the keywords "Budget Speech" (in English) and *Yùsuàn àn* (in Chinese). *Ming Pao* and the *South China Morning Post* were chosen as they are the two major Chinese and English newspapers in Hong Kong

(2) The news articles coded for Singapore were obtained from the news archives of *Lianhe Zaobao* and *The Straits Times*, which were downloaded from the NewsLink platform by searching for the keywords "Budget Speech" (in English) and "*Yùsuàn àn*" (in Chinese). *Lianhe Zaobao* and *The Straits Times* were chosen as they are the two major Chinese and English newspapers in Singapore

Research Findings

Vertical Comparison of Budgetary Demand in Hong Kong

The findings indicated that there was no significant difference for most of the budgetary demand indicators across both surplus and deficit years in Hong Kong, meaning that the overall dynamics of deficit politics and surplus politics in Hong Kong are broadly similar (Table 6.5).

Table 6.2 Operationalization of indicators of budgetary output for Hong Kong and Singapore

Tax	*Expenditure*
• Year-over-year percentage change of estimated total government taxation revenue (estimated amount as expressed in Hong Kong dollars/Singapore dollars in the respective annual Budget Speeches).	• Year-over-year percentage of estimated total government expenditure (estimated amount as expressed in Hong Kong dollars/Singapore dollars in the respective annual Budget Speeches).

Table 6.3 Comparison of the empirical pattern of budgetary demand in Hong Kong and Singapore

Vertical comparison	*Horizontal comparison*
• *Vertical comparison of budgetary demand within Hong Kong*: Is the empirical pattern of budgetary demand (as expressed in the three indicators of "media salience," "published opinion," and "politicization of public debate") in Hong Kong in deficit years and surplus years *similar or dissimilar?*	• *Horizontal comparison of budgetary demand between Hong Kong and Singapore in their deficit years*: Is the empirical pattern of budgetary demand (as expressed in the three indicators of "media salience," "published opinion," and "politicization of public debate") between Hong Kong and Singapore in their deficit years *similar or dissimilar?*
• *Vertical comparison of budgetary demand within Singapore*: Is the empirical pattern of budgetary demand (as expressed in the three indicators of "media salience," "published opinion," and "politicization of public debate") in Singapore in deficit years and surplus years *similar or dissimilar?*	• *Horizontal comparison of budgetary demand between Hong Kong and Singapore in their surplus years*: Is the empirical pattern of budgetary demand (as expressed in the three indicators of "media salience," "published opinion," and "politicization of public debate") between Hong Kong and Singapore in their surplus years *similar or dissimilar?*

The number of tax-related and reserve-related news articles ("media salience"), as well as the degree of opinionated debate on tax-related, expenditure-related, and reserve-related subjects ("politicization of debate"), was statistically similar in both deficit and surplus years, meaning that the cycles of budget deficits and surpluses did not have a significant effect on these variables. Taking the number of reserve-related news articles ("media salience") as an example, there were constant debates among party politicians, scholars, and experts on whether the government should spend or keep its reserves, resulting in a similar empirical pattern across both deficit and surplus years. The major exception to this overall

Table 6.4 Comparison of the correlation between budgetary demand and budgetary output in Hong Kong and Singapore

Vertical comparison	*Horizontal comparison*
• *Vertical comparison of the correlation between budgetary demand and budgetary output within Hong Kong*: Are budgetary demands *correlated* to the respective budgetary output of the Hong Kong government throughout deficit years and surplus years?	• *Horizontal comparison of the correlation between budgetary demand and budgetary output in Hong Kong and Singapore in their deficit years*: Is the correlation between the budgetary demand and the budgetary output in Hong Kong *stronger* than that of the Singapore government in their deficit years?
• *Vertical comparison of the correlation between budgetary demand and budgetary output within Singapore*: Are budgetary demands *correlated* to the respective budgetary output of the Singapore government throughout deficit years and surplus years?	• *Horizontal comparison of the correlation between budgetary demand and budgetary output in Hong Kong and Singapore in their surplus years*: Is the correlation between the budgetary demand and the budgetary output in Hong Kong *stronger* than that of the Singapore government in their surplus years?

empirical pattern is that the number of expenditure-related news articles ("media salience") was more salient in deficit years than surplus years, indicating that there was more extensive media coverage on the government expenditure item in times of budget deficit.

The empirical findings also indicated that there were significant differences in the claims on tax and expenditure ("published opinion") in both surplus and deficit years in Hong Kong. For the tax claim, there were stronger claims for offering tax breaks in surplus years such as demanding lower salary tax rates, higher personal allowances, and tax rebates, while there were stronger claims against offering tax breaks (including preservation of the status quo or more taxes) in deficit years such as opposing the introduction of sales tax. For the expenditure claim, there were stronger claims for increasing expenditure in surplus years such as asking for increases in social welfare and public health expenses, while there were stronger claims against increasing expenditure (including preservation of the status quo or less expenditure) in deficit years such as requesting for control of civil service pay and staff establishment.

Table 6.5 Vertical comparison of budgetary demand in Hong Kong

		N	Mean	Median	Mann–Whitney U	*p*
Media salience of "tax"	Surplus years	13	0.34	0.33	6.00	0.069
	Deficit years	3	0.46	0.46		
Media salience of "expenditure"	Surplus years	13	0.20	0.18	0.00*	0.008
	Deficit years	3	0.34	0.35		
Media salience of "reserves"	Surplus years	13	0.09	0.08	7.00	0.087
	Deficit years	3	0.13	0.12		
Politicization of debate of "tax"	Surplus years	13	1.74	1.66	6.00	0.069
	Deficit years	3	1.33	1.32		
Politicization of debate of "expenditure"	Surplus years	13	0.78	0.73	16.00	0.638
	Deficit years	3	0.67	0.71		
Politicization of debate of "reserves"	Surplus years	13	0.73	0.59	12.00	0.313
	Deficit years	3	0.49	0.51		
Published opinion of "tax"	Surplus years	13	0.24	0.26	0.00*	0.009
	Deficit years	3	-0.60	-0.55		

(*continued*)

Table 6.5 (continued)

Published opinion of "expenditu re"	Surplus years	13	0.20	0.26	0.00*	0.009
	Deficit years	3	-0.90	0.92		
Published opinion of "reserves"	Surplus years	13	0.26	0.38	10.00	0.201
	Deficit years	3	-0.21	-0.43		

Note: Indicators showing significant statistical difference according to the Mann–Whitney U test are marked with * (i.e. $p < 0.05$)(

Vertical Comparison of Budgetary Demand in Singapore

The findings indicated that there was no significant difference for most of the budgetary demand indicators across both surplus and deficit years in Singapore, meaning that the overall dynamics of deficit politics and surplus politics in Singapore are broadly similar (Table 6.6).

The number of tax-related, expenditure-related, and reserve-related news articles ("media salience"), the degree of opinionated debate on tax-related and expenditure-related subjects ("politicization of debate"), as well as the ratio of positive and negative claims on tax and reserve ("published opinion") were statistically similar across deficit and surplus years, meaning that the cycles of budget deficits and surpluses did not have a significant effect on these variables. Taking the number of tax-related news articles ("media salience") as an example, there were constant debates within Singaporean society on how to increase economic competitiveness through taxation reforms, resulting in a similar empirical pattern across both deficit and surplus years. There were two major exceptions to this overall empirical pattern. First, the degree of opinionated debate on reserve-related subjects ("politicization of debate") was more contested in surplus years than deficit years, indicating that there was more intense debate on the government's reserve in times of budget surplus. Second, there was a stronger claim for increasing expenditure in surplus years and a stronger claim against increasing expenditure (including preservation of the status quo or less expenditure) in deficit years (i.e. "published opinion").

Table 6.6 Vertical comparison of budgetary demand in Singapore

		N	Mean	Median	Mann–Whitney U	*p*
Media salience of "tax"	Surplus years	10	0.40	0.41	26.50	0.704
	Deficit years	6	0.41	0.43		
Media salience of "expenditure"	Surplus years	10	0.17	0.17	25.0	0.586
	Deficit years	6	0.19	0.14		
Media salience of "reserves"	Surplus years	10	0.06	0.05	15.0	0.101
	Deficit years	6	0.07	0.08		
Politicization of debate of "tax"	Surplus years	10	1.19	1.13	18.50	0.211
	Deficit years	6	1.36	1.38		
Politicization of debate of "expenditure"	Surplus years	10	0.22	0.15	28.50	0.870
	Deficit years	6	0.31	0.24		
Politicization of debate of "reserves"	Surplus years	10	0.48	0.42	5.50*	0.008
	Deficit years	6	0.25	0.23		
Published opinion of "tax"	Surplus years	10	0.49	0.54	29.50	0.957
	Deficit years	6	0.50	0.45		

(*continued*)

Table 6.6 (continued)

Published opinion of "expenditure"	Surplus years	10	0.43	0.47	5.00*	0.007
	Deficit years	6	-0.10	0.00		
Published opinion of "reserves"	Surplus years	10	0.27	0.27	15.00	0.096
	Deficit years	6	0.75	0.84		

Note: Indicators showing significant statistical difference according to the Mann–Whitney U test are marked with * (i.e. $p < 0.05$)

Horizontal Comparison of Budgetary Demand Between Hong Kong and Singapore in Their Deficit Years

The findings pointed that there was no significant difference between Hong Kong and Singapore in terms of "media salience" during deficit years, while the deficit politics in Hong Kong is generally more dynamic than that of Singapore as measured by "politicization of debate" and "published opinion" (Table 6.7).

The degree of opinionated debate on expenditure-related and reserve-related subjects ("politicization of debate") in Hong Kong was statistically higher than in Singapore, indicating that there were more intensified debates in Hong Kong in deficit years. Taking the degree of opinionated debate on expenditure-related subjects ("politicization of debate") as an example, in Hong Kong, there were heated debates on cutting government expenditure through privatization, civil service pay-cut, and establishment reduction in deficit years, while in Singapore, such debates were less intense. The ratio of positive and negative claims on tax, expenditure, and reserve ("published opinion") between Hong Kong and Singapore were all statistically dissimilar, with Singapore being more divided in terms of expenditure and Hong Kong being more divided in terms of reserve claims.

Table 6.7 Horizontal comparison of budgetary demand in Hong Kong and Singapore in their deficit years

		N	Mean	Median	Mann–Whitney U	*p*
Media salience of "tax"	Hong Kong	3	0.46	0.46	6.50	0.517
	Singapore	6	0.41	0.43		
Media salience of "expenditure"	Hong Kong	3	0.34	0.35	3.50	0.154
	Singapore	6	0.19	0.14		
Media salience of "reserves"	Hong Kong	3	0.13	0.12	1.50	0.052
	Singapore	6	0.07	0.08		
Politicization of debate of "tax"	Hong Kong	3	1.33	1.32	8.50	0.897
	Singapore	6	1.36	1.38		
Politicization of debate of "expenditure"	Hong Kong	3	0.67	0.71	1.00*	0.039
	Singapore	6	0.31	0.24		
Politicization of debate of "reserves"	Hong Kong	3	0.49	0.51	0.00*	0.020
	Singapore	6	0.25	0.23		
Published opinion of "tax"	Hong Kong	3	-0.60	-0.55	0.00*	0.020
	Singapore	6	0.50	0.45		

(*continued*)

Table 6.7 (continued)

Published opinion of "expenditure"	Hong Kong	3	-0.90	-0.92	0.00*	0.018
	Singapore	6	-0.10	0		
Published opinion of "reserves"	Hong Kong	3	-0.21	-0.43	0.50*	0.025
	Singapore	6	0.75	0.84		

Note: Indicators showing significant statistical difference according to the Mann–Whitney U test are marked with * (i.e. $p < 0.05$)

Horizontal Comparison of Budgetary Demand Between Hong Kong and Singapore in Their Surplus Years

The findings indicated that there was a significant difference for half of the budgetary demand indicators between Hong Kong and Singapore in surplus years, with the surplus politics in Hong Kong being generally more dynamic than that of Singapore (Table 6.8).

The number of reserve-related news articles ("media salience") and the degree of opinionated debate on tax-related and expenditure-related subjects ("politicization of debate") in Hong Kong was statistically higher than in Singapore, indicating that there was more media coverage and more intensified debates in Hong Kong in times of budget surplus. Taking the number of reserve-related news articles ("media salience") as an example, in Hong Kong, the level of government reserves was opened to the public and brought about heated debates on whether government reserves should be spent or kept in times of surplus; in Singapore, the level of government reserves was undisclosed to the public, making it difficult for society to debate the handling of government reserves. The ratio of positive and negative claims on tax, expenditure, and reserve ("published opinion") between Hong Kong and Singapore was statistically similar.

Table 6.8 Horizontal comparison of budgetary demand in Hong Kong and Singapore in their surplus years

		N	Mean	Median	Mann–Whitney U	*p*
Media salience of “tax”	Hong Kong	13	0.34	0.33	46.50	0.251
	Singapore	10	0.40	0.41		
Media salience of “expenditure”	Hong Kong	13	0.20	0.18	39.00	0.105
	Singapore	10	0.17	0.17		
Media salience of “reserves”	Hong Kong	13	0.09	0.08	18.00*	0.003
	Singapore	10	0.06	0.05		
Politicization of debate of “tax”	Hong Kong	13	1.74	1.66	17.50*	0.003
	Singapore	10	1.19	1.13		
Politicization of debate of “expenditure”	Hong Kong	13	0.78	0.73	3.00*	< 0.001
	Singapore	10	0.22	0.15		
Politicization of debate of “reserves”	Hong Kong	13	0.73	0.59	40.00	0.121
	Singapore	10	0.48	0.42		
Published opinion of “tax”	Hong Kong	13	0.24	0.26	33.50	0.051
	Singapore	10	0.49	0.54		
Published opinion of “expenditure”	Hong Kong	13	0.20	0.26	44.50	0.203
	Singapore	10	0.43	0.47		

(*continued*)

Table 6.8 (continued)

Published opinion of "reserves"	Hong Kong	13	0.26	0.38	61.50	0.828
	Singapore	10	0.27	0.27		

Note: Indicators showing significant statistical difference according to the Mann–Whitney U test are marked with * (i.e. $p < 0.05$)

Testing the Correlation Between Budgetary Demand and Budgetary Output

The findings indicated that there was generally no correlation between the claims on tax and expenditure ("published opinion") and the respective budgetary output of both the Hong Kong and the Singapore governments, irrespective of the ups and downs in budget cycles (Table 6.9). In other words, both the Hong Kong and Singapore governments were far from responsive to the published opinion of non-governmental actors when formulating their budgets. The only exception to this overall empirical pattern was the statistical correlation between the expenditure claims of non-governmental actors in Singapore and the respective budgetary output of the Singapore government throughout deficit years and surplus years.

Further testing was conducted to assess whether general elections, Chief Executive elections in Hong Kong and parliamentary general elections in Singapore, have any implication on the responsiveness of the Hong Kong and Singaporean governments to the published opinion of non-governmental actors when formulating their budgets.

The findings indicated that there was generally no correlation between the claims on tax and expenditure ("published opinion") and the respective budgetary output of both the Hong Kong and the Singapore governments, irrespective of the election and non-election years (Table 6.10). The only two exceptions to this overall empirical pattern were the correlation between the tax claims of non-governmental actors in Hong Kong and the respective budgetary output of the Hong Kong government in election years, and the correlation between the expenditure claims of non-governmental actors in Hong Kong and the respective budgetary output of the Singaporean government in election years.

Table 6.9 Comparisons of the correlation between budgetary demand and budgetary output

	Pearson's correlation	*p*
Vertical comparisons		
Correlation between *"published opinion" of tax* and the respective *budgetary output of the Hong Kong government* throughout deficit years and surplus years	0.299	0.26
Correlation between *"published opinion" of expenditure* and the respective *budgetary output of the Hong Kong government* throughout deficit years and surplus years	0.19	0.49
Correlation between *"published opinion" of tax* and the respective *budgetary output of the Singapore government* throughout deficit years and surplus years	-0.39	0.14
Correlation between *"published opinion" of expenditure* and the respective *budgetary output of the Singapore government* throughout deficit years and surplus years	*0.68	0.003
Horizontal comparisons		
Correlation between *"published opinion" of tax* and the respective *budgetary output of the Hong Kong government* in surplus years	0.07	0.83
Correlation between *"published opinion" of tax* and the respective *budgetary output of the Singapore government* in surplus years	-0.44	0.20
Correlation between *"published opinion" of expenditure* and the respective *budgetary output of the Hong Kong government* in surplus years	0.45	0.13
Correlation between *"published opinion" of expenditure* and the respective *budgetary output of the Singapore government* in surplus years	0.56	0.9
Correlation between *"published opinion" of tax* and the respective *budgetary output of the Hong Kong government* in deficit years	0.57	0.62
Correlation between *"published opinion" of tax* and the respective *budgetary output of the Singapore government* in deficit years	-0.42	0.41
Correlation between *"published opinion" of expenditure* and the respective *budgetary output of the Hong Kong government* in deficit years	0.09	0.94
Correlation between *"published opinion" of expenditure* and the respective *budgetary output of the Singapore government* in deficit years	-0.51	0.31

Note: Indicators showing significant Pearson's correlation are marked with * (i.e. $p < 0.05$)

Table 6.10 Comparisons of the correlation between budgetary demand and budgetary output (breakdown by election and non-election years)

	Pearson's correlation	*p*
Correlation between *"published opinion" of tax* and the respective *budgetary output of the Hong Kong government* in election years	0.994*	0.006
Correlation between *"published opinion" of tax* and the respective *budgetary output of the Singapore government* in election years	-0.521	0.479
Correlation between *"published opinion" of expenditure* and the respective *budgetary output of the Hong Kong government* in election years	0.186	0.814
Correlation between *"published opinion" of expenditure* and the respective *budgetary output of the Singapore government* in election years	0.455	0.545
Correlation between *"published opinion" of tax* and the respective *budgetary output of the Hong Kong government* in non-election years	-0.041	0.898
Correlation between *"published opinion" of tax* and the respective *budgetary output of the Singapore government* in non-election years	-0.378	0.225
Correlation between *"published opinion" of expenditure* and the respective *budgetary output of the Hong Kong government* in non-election years	0.280	0.377
Correlation between *"published opinion" of expenditure* and the respective *budgetary output of the Singapore government* in non-election years	0.742*	0.006

Notes: (1) Indicators showing significant Pearson's correlation are marked with * (i.e. $p < 0.05$)

(2) In the case of Hong Kong, election years are referred to the Chief Executive elections held in 2002, 2005, 2007, and 2012; while in the case of Singapore, election years are referred to parliamentary general elections held in 2001, 2006, 2011, and 2015

Observations and Explanations

To sum up, there were three major observations and explanations from the above empirical patterns of Hong Kong's and Singapore's deficit politics and surplus politics.

First, surplus politics is no less dynamic than deficit politics and consistent budget surpluses are a source of recurring budgetary conflicts the same as the cases of consistent budget deficits. As shown in the vertical comparison of budgetary demand in Hong Kong and Singapore (Tables 6.5 and 6.6), there was no significant difference on the empirical pattern of "media salience" and "politicization of debate" across their ups and downs in budget cycles. This finding conforms with Wildavsky's (2004) hypothesis that surpluses will bring about budgetary conflicts basically the same as deficits. Still, the exact budgetary claims on tax, expenditure, and reserve in deficit and surplus years could be different, as shown in the changing ratio of the positive and negative "published opinion" in Hong Kong and Singapore over the years.

Second, both deficit politics and surplus politics are structured by the larger political system, including the characteristics of media and opposition politics. As shown in the horizontal comparison of budgetary demand in Hong Kong and Singapore (Tables 6.7 and 6.8), both deficit politics and surplus politics in Hong Kong are generally more dynamic than that of Singapore. This finding conforms with existing literature about Hong Kong's more competitive media and opposition politics, where non-governmental groups from pro-democracy camps to pro-China camps are more prepared to challenge the Hong Kong government over economic-livelihood issues, including budgets (Ma, 2012). Comparatively, Singapore's media and opposition politics are well-known to be less dynamic as a result of decades of the one-party rule by the People's Action Party, with legislators from the opposition parties being less critical of the government's budgets (Dayley, 2020: 251).

Third, the responsiveness of governments to the budgetary demands of non-governmental actors is not only structured by the nature of the political regimes, but also by constitutional rules and economic growth strategies. It is comprehensible that the limited correlation between the published opinion of non-governmental actors in Hong Kong and Singapore and the budgetary output of their governments (Tables 6.9 and 6.10) is far from being only the result of the non-democratic regimes of the two city-states, with Hong Kong being a liberal authoritarian regime and Singapore being an electoral authoritarian regime (Case, 2008; Fong, 2016). Constitutional rules matter. Both Hong Kong and Singapore have codified the principles of fiscal conservativism into their constitutional documents, constitutionally constraining the scope of their governments in budget allocations throughout deficit years and surplus years. Therefore, striving for a balanced budget is always the rule for the Hong Kong and Singapore governments when preparing for their annual budgets (Scott, 2010: 152; Sugimoto & Tan, 2011), making their budgetary outputs less responsive to the changing budgetary demand, regardless of the ups and downs of budget cycles. Economic growth strategies matter, too. As city-state financial centres, both the Hong Kong and Singaporean governments have put great emphasis on attracting local and foreign capitals for their dynamic financial industries. Fiscal conservatism, which underscores the small, efficient public sectors of Hong Kong and Singapore, is an important component of their growth strategies as international financial centres (Goodhart & Dai, 2003: 15; Woo, 2007: 84).

As a consequence of both constitutional rules and economic growth strategies, budgets in Hong Kong and Singapore are not primarily formulated to satisfy changing budgetary demands of the society, but they are habitually manipulated to exhibit the fundamental principles of fiscal conservatism—for example, Hong Kong government has, for many years, habitually made conservative economic and budget forecasts, aiming to provide a cover for its restrained welfare spending, with the actual budgets always turned out to be huge surpluses in the next fiscal year (Economist Intelligence Unit, 2018); Similarly, the Singaporean government is also found to have habitually downplayed its revenues such as land sales and played up many expenditures that are by nature capital top-ups to endowment and trust funds. Such budgeting practices have resulted in either the under-statement of budget surpluses or over-statement of budget deficits (The Straits Times, 2015). If "budgets are reflections of priorities, and budget change distributions reflect changing priorities" according to the general budgetary laws as authoritatively advanced by Baumgartner et al. (2009), then it is clear that the budget priorities of the Hong Kong and Singaporean government remain consistently based upon fiscal conservatism, regardless of cyclical changes in deficits and surpluses. In other words, Hong Kong and Singapore have effectively overcome the propensity of over-spending in boom years and over-cutting in bust years confronting many fiscal jurisdictions worldwide (Thompson et al., 2017).

Conclusion

This chapter is the first comparative case study to explore the dynamics of deficit politics and surplus politics, using Hong Kong and Singapore as binary cases. It is important to note that budgeting scholars are only at the beginning of a long process of comparatively studying deficit politics and surplus politics.

As stated in the introduction, there are quite a number of countries and regions that have experienced cycles of both budget deficits and budget surpluses over the years. Building upon the idea of media content analysis, the comparative framework developed in this article has the potential to be developed into large-N comparative studies across fiscal jurisdictions of varying political, socio-economic, and cultural backgrounds. The development of such a comparative framework and its preliminary application in Hong Kong and Singapore echoed the calls of Jensen et al. (2018) to empirically study public budgeting through statistical modelling and pointed to a new line of empirical inquiry into the comparison of deficit politics and surplus politics.

Yet, the volume of labour-intensive coding tasks will be tremendous and practical constraints such as language differences and availabilities of online news archives are unavoidable, if the comparative framework is to be applied to a wider group of fiscal jurisdictions. Despite the challenges, comparative budgeting scholars have much to study in this direction of comparing deficit politics and surplus politics.

Further Readings

- Wildavsky, A. B. (2004). *The New Politics of the Budgetary Process.* London, UK: Pearson/Longman.

A classical account of the theories of budgetary politics, with analysis of both deficit politics and surplus politics.

- Cheung, A. B. L. (2006). Budgetary Reforms in Two City States: Impact on the Central Budget Agency in Hong Kong and Singapore. *International Review of Administrative Sciences, 72*(3), 341–361.

A classical comparative study of the budgetary politics of Hong Kong and Singapore.

- Asher, M. G., Bali, A. S., & Kwan C. Y. (2015). Public Financial Management in Singapore: Key Characteristics and Prospects. *The Singapore Economic Review, 60*(3), 1550032–18.

A concise, comprehensive account of public budgeting in Singapore, including its institutions, practices, and composition of government revenues and expenditures.

Bibliography

Asher, M. G. (1989). Fiscal System and Practices in Singapore. In Mukul G. Asher (Ed.), *Fiscal System and Practices in ASEAN Countries* (pp. 131–83). Singapore: Institute of Southeast Asian Studies.

Asher, M. G., Bali, A. S., & Kwan, C. Y. (2015). Public Financial Management in Singapore: Key Characteristics and Prospects. *The Singapore Economic Review, 60*(03), 1550032–1550018.

Baumgartner Jones, B. D., Breunig, F. R., Wlezien, C., Soroka, C., Foucault, S., François, M., Green, A., Pedersen, C., Koski, C., John, P., et al. (2009). A General Empirical Law of Public Budgets: A Comparative Analysis. *American Journal of Political Science, 53*(4), 855–873. https://doi.org/10.1111/j.1540-5907.2009.00405.x.

Blöndal, J. R. (2006). Budgeting in Singapore. *OECD Journal on Budgeting, 6*(1), 45–86.

Brendon, P. (2007). *The Decline and Fall of the British Empire 1781–1997.* Jonathan Cape Bright.

Case, W. (2008). Hybrid Politics and New Competitiveness: Hong Kong's 2007 Chief Executive Election. *East Asia, 25*(4), 365–388.

Cheung, A. B. L. (2005). *Budgeting for Results or Budgeting for Politics: Budget Reforms, Fiscal Stability and Distributional Politics in Hong Kong Re-Examineds.* A Paper Presented in the 61st Congress of the International Institute of Public Finance Jeju, Korea, 22–25 August 2005.

Cheung, A. B. L. (2006). Budgetary Reforms in Two City States: Impact on the Central Budget Agency in Hong Kong and Singapore. *International Review of Administrative Sciences, 72*(3), 341–361.

Dayley, R. (2020). *Southeast Asia in the New International Era* (8th ed.). Routledge.

Economist Intelligence Unit. (2018). How to Take Advantage of a Huge Fiscal Surplus? February 28. Retrieved February 12, 2021, from http://country.eiu.com/article.aspx?articleid=896476473&country=hong+kong&topic=economy&subtopic=_4

Fong, B. C. H. (2015). The Politics of Budget Surpluses: The Case of China's HKSAR. *International Review of Administrative Sciences, 81*(1), 134–157.

Fong, B. C. H. (2016). In-Between Liberal Authoritarianism and Electoral Authoritarianism: Hong Kong's Democratization Under Chinese Sovereignty, 1997–2016. *Democratization, 24*(4), 724–750.

Fong, B. C. H. (2019). Democratization and Budget Openness: Evidences from Hong Kong, Macao, and Taiwan. *International Review of Administrative Sciences.* Article First Published Online: 8 July 2019. https://doi.org/10.1177/0020852319845453

Fong, B. C. H. (2020). Practicing Autonomy Within a Communist State: Hong Kong's Autonomy from Handover to Anti-Extradition Bill Movement, 1997 to 2019. *Communist and Post-Communist Studies, 53*(4), 68–90.

Goodhart, C., & Dai, L. (2003). *Intervention to Save Hong Kong: The Authorities' Counter – Speculation in Financial Markets.* Oxford University Press.

Goodstadt, L. F. (2009). *Uneasy Partners: The Conflict Between Public Interest and Private Profit Interest in Hong Kong.* Hong Kong University Press.

Guess, G., & Leloup, L. (2021). *Comparative Public Budgeting: Global Perspectives on Taxing And Spending.* Albany: State University of New York Press.

Hague, R., & Harrop, M. (2013). *Comparative Government and Politics: An Introduction.* Palgrave Macmillan.

Ide, E., & Park, G. (2015). *Deficits and Debt in Industrialized Democracies*. Routledge.

Imbeau, L., & Pétry, F. (2004). The Political Economy of Public Deficits. In L. Imbeau & F. Pétry (Eds.), *Politics, Institutions, and Fiscal Policy: Deficits and Surpluses in Federated States* (pp. 1–19). Lexington Books.

Jensen, J. L., Mortensen, P. B., & Serritzlew, S. (2019). A Comparative Distributional Method for Public Administration Illustrated Using Public Budget Data. *Journal of Public Administration Research and Theory, 29*(3), 460–473. https://doi.org/10.1093/jopart/muy056.

Kettl, D. F. (2003). *Deficit Politics: The Search for Balance in American Politics*. Longman.

Ma, N. (2012). Political Parties and Elections. In W. M. Lam, P. L. T. Lui, & W. Wong (Eds.), *Contemporary Hong Kong Government and Politics* (pp. 159–177). Hong Kong University Press.

Morgan, I. W. (2009). *The Age of Deficits: Presidents and Unbalanced Budgets from Jimmy Carter to George W. Bush*. University Press of Kansas.

Oehl, B., Schaffer, L. M., & Bernauer, T. (2016). How to Measure Public Demand for Policies when There is No Appropriate Survey Data? *Journal of Public Policy, 37*(2), 1–32.

Peters, B. G. (2013). *Strategies for Comparative Research in Political Science*. Palgrave Macmillan.

Posner, P. L. (2013). *The Politics of Fiscal Austerity: Democracies and Hard Choices*. OECD Publishing.

Rubin, I. (2020). *The Politics of Public Budgeting: Getting and Spending, Borrowing and Balancing* (9th ed.). Sage/CQ Press.

Scott, I. (2010). *The Public Sector in Hong Kong*. Hong Kong University Press.

Sugimoto, I., & Tan, E. C. (2011). Government Fiscal Behaviour and Economic Growth of Singapore in the Twentieth Century. *The Singapore Economic Review, 56*(1), 19–40.

The Straits Times. (2015). Budget 2015: In Deficit, Yet Very Prudent at Heart. March 7. Retrieved February 12, 2021, from https://www.straitstimes.com/opinion/budget-2015-in-deficit-yet-very-prudent-at-heart

Thompson, F., Pierson, K., Hand, M. L., & Dothan, M. U. (2017). Is a Good Normative Model of Public Spending Run Backward a Good Positive Model? *Public Budgeting & Finance, 37*(2), 35–57. https://doi.org/10.1111/pbaf.12121

Wang, X. H. (2014). *Financial Management in the Public Sector: Tools, Applications, and Cases* (3rd ed.). M.E. Sharpe, Inc.

Wildavsky, A. B. (1986). *Budgeting: A Comparative Theory of the Budgeting Process*. Transaction Publishers.

Wildavsky, A. B. (2004). *The New Politics of the Budgetary Process*. Pearson/Longman.

Woo, J. J. (2007). *3-In-1: Governing a Global Financial Centre*. World Scientific.

Appendices: Profiles of Hong Kong Public Budgeting

Annual Budget Cycle[1]

Since the 1990s, the annual budget cycle of the Hong Kong government has been institutionalized as the "Resource Allocation Exercise" (RAE). Overseen by the Star Chamber, the RAE involves all controlling officers from different policy bureaux and departments. The existing annual budget cycle of the Hong Kong government is graphically presented as follows.

[1] The annual budget cycle presented in this section was based upon my anonymous interviews with several government officials conducted in 2019.

B. C. H. Fong, *Hong Kong Public Budgeting*, Hong Kong Studies Reader Series, https://doi.org/10.1007/978-981-16-5363-6

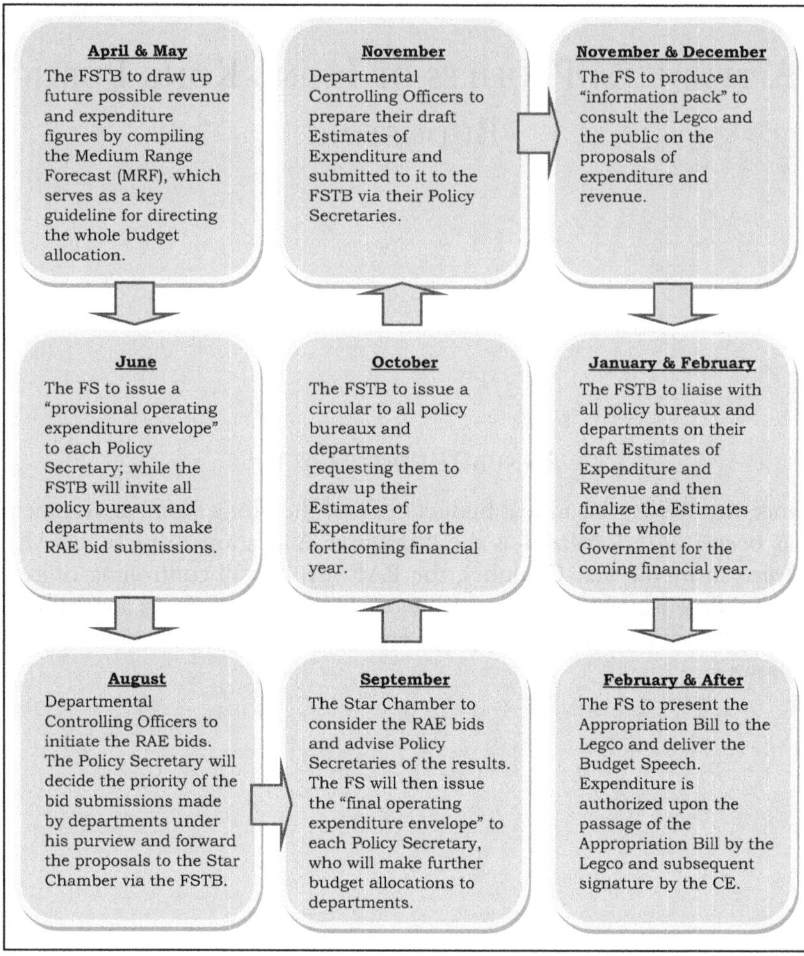

Note: FS denotes Financial Secretary; FSTB denotes Financial Services and Treasury Bureau; Legco denotes the Legislative Council; CE denotes the Chief Executive

Government Accounts[2]

The consolidated accounts of the Hong Kong government are comprised of the General Revenue Account (GRA) and nine special funds established under the Public Finance Ordinance—namely Capital Works Reserve Fund, Capital Investment Fund, Civil Service Pension Reserve Fund, Disaster Relief Fund, Innovation and Technology Fund, Land Fund, Loan Fund, Lotteries Fund, and Bond Fund. All government's financial activities are strictly conducted through these accounts and funds.

Overall, the GRA is the main operating account of the Hong Kong government, through which the day-to-day government expenditure payments and revenue collection are controlled, while the nine special funds were established under the Public Finance Ordinance based upon designated policy purposes.

Account	*Official purpose*
General revenue account	"The General Revenue Account is the main operating account through which the Government's finances are controlled."
Capital works reserve fund	"The Capital Works Reserve Fund was established with effect from 1 April 1982 by Resolution of the Legislative Council on 20 January 1982 for the purpose of financing the Public Works Programme and the acquisition of land."
Capital investment fund	"On 1 April 1990, the Legislative Council established the Capital Investment Fund by Resolution for the purpose of financing investments in the Mass Transit Railway Corporation (which became MTR Corporation Limited on 30 June 2000), the Kowloon-Canton Railway Corporation, the Hong Kong Housing Authority, the New Hong Kong Tunnel Company Limited and such other bodies as the Finance Committee may specify. On 6 November 1991, the Legislative Council passed an amendment to the Resolution to include provisions for government borrowings to be credited to the Fund and for repayments, and payments of interest and expenses relating to such borrowings, to be made from the Fund."
Civil service pension reserve fund	"On 25 January 1995, the Legislative Council established the Civil Service Pension Reserve Fund by Resolution to provide a reserve to meet payment of civil service pensions in the unlikely event that the Government cannot meet its liabilities for such payment from the General Revenue Account."

[2] The structure of the government accounts and their official purposes were extracted and reprinted from the official budget website of the Hong Kong government, available at: https://www.budget.gov.hk (Accessed 12 June 2021).

Disaster relief fund	"On 1 December 1993, the Legislative Council established the Disaster Relief Fund by Resolution to provide a ready mechanism for Hong Kong to respond swiftly to international appeals for humanitarian aid in relief of disasters that occur outside Hong Kong."
Innovation and technology fund	"The Innovation and Technology Fund was established on 30 June 1999 by Resolution of the Legislative Council to finance projects to help promote innovation and technology upgrading in manufacturing and service industries. These efforts will contribute to increased productivity and enhanced competitiveness, and hence will be conducive to the long-term economic development of Hong Kong."
Land fund	"The Land Fund was established on 1 July 1997 by Resolution of the Provisional Legislative Council to receive and holdall of the assets, including all accounts receivable, net of expenses, transferred from the Hong Kong Special Administrative Region Government Land Fund."
Loan fund	"On 1 April 1990, the Legislative Council established the Loan Fund by Resolution to assume the functions of the Development Loan Fund and the Student Loan Fund. The Development Loan Fund had been used to finance development schemes in Hong Kong through loans and advances. The Student Loan Fund had been used to finance loans to students at selected post-secondary institutions."
Lotteries fund	"The Lotteries Fund was established on 30June1965 by Resolution of the Legislative Council for the purpose of financing social welfare services by grants, loans and advances. The Fund took over the unspent funds raised by lotteries held under the Government Lotteries Ordinance 1962. Between 1965 and 1975 it received the net proceeds of government lotteries held during those years. The old style lotteries were changed to the Mark Six Lottery in September1975. The Fund is now mainly funded from this source."
Bond fund	"The Bond Fund was established by the Resolution passed by the Legislative Council under section 29 of the Public Finance Ordinance (Cap. 2) on 8 July 2009 in connection with the implementation of the Government Bond Programme to promote the further and sustainable development of the bond market in Hong Kong. The Programme can provide more diversified investment products and avenues for financing to attract more overseas capital, and reinforce Hong Kong's position as an international financial centre. The Programme consists of an institutional part and a retail part. The Fund does not form part of the fiscal reserves and is managed separately from other Government accounts. The Fund is placed with the Exchange Fund for investment purposes and attracts investment income on the basis of the "fixed rate" sharing arrangement applicable to the fiscal reserves."

Government Estimates[3]

The Government Estimates are comprised of Volumes I and II, which contain all the details of the expenditure and revenues of the Hong Kong government. Volume I of the Government Estimates contains the expenditure analysis of the General Revenue Account by Head, with Controlling Officers' Reports, details of expenditure by Subhead, and Commitments for each Head of Expenditure provided. Volume II contains the expenditure analysis of the nine special funds, with their statutory backgrounds, purposes, and details of expenditure provided. The structures of the latest 2021–2022 Government Estimates are presented and reproduced as follows.

Volume I: General revenue account

Expenditure analysis by head

Head 21 – Chief Executive's Office
Head 22 – Agriculture, Fisheries and Conservation Department
Head 25 – Architectural Services Department
Head 24 – Audit Commission
Head 23 – Auxiliary Medical Service
Head 82 – Buildings Department
Head 26 – Census and Statistics Department
Head 27 – Civil Aid Service
Head 28 – Civil Aviation Department
Head 33 – Civil Engineering and Development Department
Head 30 – Correctional Services Department
Head 31 – Customs and Excise Department
Head 37 – Department of Health
Head 92 – Department of Justice
Head 39 – Drainage Services Department
Head 42 – Electrical and Mechanical Services Department
Head 44 – Environmental Protection Department
Head 45 – Fire Services Department
Head 49 – Food and Environmental Hygiene Department
Head 46 – General Expenses of the Civil Service
Head 166 – Government Flying Service
Head 48 – Government Laboratory
Head 59 – Government Logistics Department
Head 51 – Government Property Agency
Head 143 – Government Secretariat: Civil Service Bureau

[3] The structure of the Government Estimates presented in this section was extracted and reprinted from the official budget website of the Hong Kong government, available at: https://www.budget.gov.hk (Accessed 12 June 2021).

Head 152 – Government Secretariat: Commerce and Economic Development Bureau (Commerce, Industry and Tourism Branch)
Head 55 – Government Secretariat: Commerce and Economic Development Bureau (Communications and Creative Industries Branch)
Head 144 – Government Secretariat: Constitutional and Mainland Affairs Bureau
Head 138 – Government Secretariat: Development Bureau (Planning and Lands Branch)
Head 159 – Government Secretariat: Development Bureau (Works Branch)
Head 156 – Government Secretariat: Education Bureau
Head 137 – Government Secretariat: Environment Bureau
Head 148 – Government Secretariat: Financial Services and the Treasury Bureau (Financial Services Branch)
Head 147 – Government Secretariat: Financial Services and the Treasury Bureau (The Treasury Branch)
Head 139 – Government Secretariat: Food and Health Bureau (Food Branch)
Head 140 – Government Secretariat: Food and Health Bureau (Health Branch)
Head 53 – Government Secretariat: Home Affairs Bureau
Head 135 – Government Secretariat: Innovation and Technology Bureau
Head 155 – Government Secretariat: Innovation and Technology Commission
Head 141 – Government Secretariat: Labour and Welfare Bureau
Head 47 – Government Secretariat: Office of the Government Chief Information Officer
Head 142 – Government Secretariat: Offices of the Chief Secretary for Administration and the Financial Secretary
Head 96 – Government Secretariat: Overseas Economic and Trade Offices
Head 151 – Government Secretariat: Security Bureau
Head 158 – Government Secretariat: Transport and Housing Bureau (Transport Branch)
Head 60 – Highways Department
Head 63 – Home Affairs Department
Head 168 – Hong Kong Observatory
Head 122 – Hong Kong Police Force
Head 62 – Housing Department
Head 70 – Immigration Department
Head 72 – Independent Commission Against Corruption
Head 121 – Independent Police Complaints Council
Head 74 – Information Services Department
Head 76 – Inland Revenue Department
Head 78 – Intellectual Property Department
Head 79 – Invest Hong Kong
Head 174 – Joint Secretariat for the Advisory Bodies on Civil Service and Judicial Salaries and Conditions of Service
Head 80 – Judiciary
Head 90 – Labour Department
Head 91 – Lands Department
Head 94 – Legal Aid Department

Head 112 – Legislative Council Commission
Head 95 – Leisure and Cultural Services Department
Head 100 – Marine Department
Head 106 – Miscellaneous Services
Head 180 – Office for Film, Newspaper and Article Administration
Head 114 – Office of The Ombudsman
Head 116 – Official Receiver's Office
Head 120 – Pensions
Head 118 – Planning Department
Head 136 – Public Service Commission Secretariat
Head 160 – Radio Television Hong Kong
Head 162 – Rating and Valuation Department
Head 163 – Registration and Electoral Office
Head 169 – Secretariat, Commissioner on Interception of Communications and Surveillance
Head 170 – Social Welfare Department
Head 181 – Trade and Industry Department
Head 186 – Transport Department
Head 188 – Treasury
Head 190 – University Grants Committee
Head 194 – Water Supplies Department
Head 173 – Working Family and Student Financial Assistance Agency
Head 184 – Transfers to Funds

Revenue analysis by head

Head 1 – Duties
Head 2 – General Rates
Head 3 – Internal Revenue
Head 4 – Motor Vehicle Taxes
Head 5 – Fines, Forfeitures and Penalties
Head 6 – Royalties and Concessions
Head 7 – Properties and Investments
Head 9 – Loans, Reimbursements, Contributions and Other Receipts
Head 10 – Utilities
Head 11 – Fees and Charges

Volume II: Fund accounts

Capital Works Reserve Fund
Capital Investment Fund
Civil Service Pension Reserve Fund
Disaster Relief Fund
Innovation and Technology Fund
Land Fund
Loan Fund
Lotteries Fund
Bond Fund

Glossary of Terms[4]

Capital expenditure. This comprises all expenditure charged to the Capital Account of the General Revenue Account, Capital Investment Fund, Capital Works Reserve Fund (including interest on government bonds and notes but excluding repayment of the bonds and notes), Disaster Relief Fund, Innovation and Technology Fund, Loan Fund and Lotteries Fund. Major items are highlighted below:

General Revenue Account
equipment, works and capital subventions of a minor nature
Capital Investment Fund
advances and equity investments
Capital Works Reserve Fund
acquisition of land
capital subventions
computerisation
interest and other expenses on government bonds and notes
major systems and equipment
Public Works Programme expenditure
Disaster Relief Fund
relief to disasters that occur outside Hong Kong
Innovation and Technology Fund
projects promoting innovation and technology upgrading in manufacturing and service industries
Loan Fund
loans made under various development schemes supported by the Government
loans to schools, teachers, students, and housing loans to civil servants, etc.
Lotteries Fund
grants, loans and advances for social welfare services

Capital surplus / (deficit). The difference between capital revenue and capital expenditure.

Capital revenue. This comprises certain revenue items in the General Revenue Account and all receipts credited to seven Funds, as highlighted below:

[4] All the terms in the glossary presented in this section were extracted and reprinted from the official budget website of the Hong Kong government, available at: https://www.budget.gov.hk (Accessed 12 June 2021).

General Revenue Account
- disposal proceeds of government quarters and other assets
- estate duty
- loan repayments received
- recovery from Housing Authority

Capital Investment Fund
- Dividends from investments
- interest on loans
- investment income
- loan repayments received
- proceeds from sale of investments

Capital Works Reserve Fund
- investment income
- land premium
- recovery from MTR Corporation Limited

Civil Service Pension Reserve Fund
- investment income

Disaster Relief Fund
- investment income

Innovation and Technology Fund
- investment income
- loan repayments received
- proceeds from sale of investments

Loan Fund
- interest on loans
- investment income
- loan repayments received
- proceeds from sale of loans

Lotteries Fund
- auctions of vehicle registration numbers
- investment income
- loan repayments received
- share of proceeds from the Mark Six Lottery

Consolidated deficit before issuance and repayment of bonds. The difference between government revenue and government expenditure.

Fiscal reserves. The accumulated balances of the General Revenue Account, Capital Investment Fund, Capital Works Reserve Fund, Civil Service Pension Reserve Fund, Disaster Relief Fund, Innovation and Technology Fund, Land Fund, Loan Fund and Lotteries Fund.

Future Fund. It is the part of the fiscal reserves which is set aside for longer-term investment with a view to securing higher investment returns for the fiscal reserves. It is a notional savings account established on 1 January 2016. It comprises the balance of the Land Fund as its initial endowment and top-ups from consolidated surpluses to be transferred from *Operating and Capital Reserves* which is the part of the fiscal reserves outside the Future Fund.

Government expenditure. The aggregate of *operating expenditure* and *capital expenditure*. Unlike *public expenditure*, it excludes expenditure by the Trading Funds and the Housing Authority.

Government revenue. The aggregate of operating revenue and capital revenue.

Operating and Capital Reserves. With the establishment of the *Future Fund*, the part of the fiscal reserves outside the Future Fund is collectively known as the Operating and Capital Reserves.

Operating expenditure. All expenditure charged to the Operating Account of the General Revenue Account and the Land Fund.

Operating revenue. This comprises all revenue credited to the General Revenue Account (except those items which are treated as capital revenue) and the Land Fund, as highlighted below:

General Revenue Account
- duties
- fines, forfeitures and penalties
- investment income
- rents and rates
- royalties and concessions
- taxes
- utilities, fees and charges

Land Fund
- investment income

Operating deficit. The difference between operating revenue and operating expenditure.

Public expenditure. *Government expenditure* plus expenditure (operating and capital) by the Trading Funds and the Housing Authority.

Transfer to Funds. Transfers between the General Revenue Account and the eight Funds (Capital Investment Fund, Capital Works Reserve Fund, Civil Service Pension Reserve Fund, Disaster Relief Fund, Innovation and Technology Fund, Land Fund, Loan Fund and Lotteries Fund) are not counted as government revenue and expenditure as these are merely internal transfers within Government's accounts.

Financial Statistics[5]

Overview (in $ million)

	Nominal GDP (calendar year) [$ million]	*Total government revenue [$ million]*	*Total government expenditure [$ million]*	*Issuance / (Repayment) of bonds and notes [$ million]*	*Surplus / (Deficit) [$ million]*	*Fiscal reserves as at end of the financial year [$ million]*
2021–2022[a]	2,859,800	591,105	727,827	35,100	(101,622)	826,154[b]
2020–2021	2,688,536	564,230	816,066	19,304	(232,532)	927,776
2019–2020	2,844,560	590,926	607,830	6329	(10,575)	1,160,308
2018–2019	2,835,119	599,774	531,825	–	67,949	1,170,883
2017–2018	2,659,384	619,837	470,863	–	148,974	1,102,934
2016–2017	2,490,438	573,124	462,052	–	111,072	953,960
2015–2016	2,398,280	450,007	435,633	–	14,374	842,888
2014–2015	2,260,005	478,668	396,183	(9688)	72,797	828,514
2013–2014	2,138,305	455,346	433,543	–	21,803	755,717
2012–2013	2,037,059	442,150	377,324	–	64,826	733,914
2011–2012	1,934,430	437,723	364,037	–	73,686	669,088
2010–2011	1,776,332	376,481	301,360	–	75,121	595,402
2009–2010	1,659,245	318,442	289,025	(3500)	25,917	520,281
2008–2009	1,707,487	316,562	312,412	(2700)	1450	494,364
2007–2008	1,650,756	358,465	234,815	–	123,650	492,914
2006–2007	1,503,351	288,014	226,863	(2550)	58,601	369,264
2005–2006	1,412,125	247,035	233,071	–	13,964	310,663
2004–2005	1,316,949	238,197	242,235	25,394	21,356	295,981
2003–2004	1,256,669	207,338	247,466	–	(40,128)	275,343
2002–2003	1,297,341	177,489	239,177	–	(61,688)	311,402
2001–2002	1,321,142	175,559	238,890	–	(63,331)	372,503
2000–2001	1,337,501	225,060	232,893	–	(7833)	430,278
1999–2000	1,285,946	232,995	223,043	–	9952	444,254
1998–1999	1,308,074	216,115	239,356	–	(23,241)	434,302
1997–1998	1,373,083	281,226	194,360	–	86,866	457,543

[a]Original estimate

[b]The forecast fiscal reserves balance as at end-March 2022 is revised to take into account the financial results in 2020–2021

[5]All the statistical tables presented in this section were extracted and reprinted from Financial Services and the Treasury Bureau's website, available at: https://www.fstb.gov.hk/tb/en/business/pub_finance/financial-statistics.htm (Accessed 12 June 2021).

Overview (as % of GDP)

	Nominal GDP (calendar year) [$ million]	*Total government revenue [% of GDP]*	*Total government expenditure [% of GDP]*	*Issuance / (Repayment) of bonds and notes [% of GDP]*	*Surplus / (Deficit) [% of GDP]*	*Fiscal reserves as at end of the financial year [% of GDP]*
2021–2022[a]	2,859,800	20.7	25.5	1.2	(3.6)	28.9[b]
2020–2021	2,688,536	21.0	30.4	0.7	(8.6)	34.5
2019–2020	2,844,560	20.8	21.4	0.2	(0.4)	40.8
2018–2019	2,835,119	21.2	18.8	–	2.4	41.3
2017–2018	2,659,384	23.3	17.7	–	5.6	41.5
2016–2017	2,490,438	23.0	18.6	–	4.5	38.3
2015–2016	2,398,280	18.8	18.2	–	0.6	35.1
2014–2015	2,260,005	21.2	17.5	(0.4)	3.2	36.7
2013–2014	2,138,305	21.3	20.3	–	1.0	35.3
2012–2013	2,037,059	21.7	18.5	–	3.2	36.0
2011–2012	1,934,430	22.6	18.8	–	3.8	34.6
2010–2011	1,776,332	21.2	17.0	–	4.2	33.5
2009–2010	1,659,245	19.2	17.4	(0.2)	1.6	31.4
2008–2009	1,707,487	18.5	18.3	(0.2)	0.1	29.0
2007–2008	1,650,756	21.7	14.2	–	7.5	29.9
2006–2007	1,503,351	19.2	15.1	(0.2)	3.9	24.6
2005–2006	1,412,125	17.5	16.5	–	1.0	22.0
2004–2005	1,316,949	18.1	18.4	1.9	1.6	22.5
2003–2004	1,256,669	16.5	19.7	–	(3.2)	21.9
2002–2003	1,297,341	13.7	18.4	–	(4.8)	24.0
2001–2002	1,321,142	13.3	18.1	–	(4.8)	28.2
2000–2001	1,337,501	16.8	17.4	–	(0.6)	32.2
1999–2000	1,285,946	18.1	17.3	–	0.8	34.5
1998–1999	1,308,074	16.5	18.3	–	(1.8)	33.2
1997–1998	1,373,083	20.5	14.2	–	6.3	33.3

[a]Original estimate

[b]The forecast fiscal reserves balance as at end-March 2022 is revised to take into account the financial results in 2020–2021

Government operating and capital revenue (in $ million)

	Operating revenue [$ million]	*Capital revenue [$ million]*	*Total government revenue [$ million]*
2021–2022[a]	470,278	120,827	591,105
2020–2021	459,305	104,925	564,230
2019–2020	433,854	157,072	590,926
2018–2019	454,416	145,358	599,774
2017–2018	442,759	177,078	619,837
2016–2017	411,727	161,397	573,124
2015–2016	381,532	68,475	450,007
2014–2015	393,934	84,734	478,668
2013–2014	355,292	100,054	455,346
2012–2013	344,606	97,544	442,150
2011–2012	339,421	98,302	437,723
2010–2011	299,800	76,681	376,481
2009–2010	262,860	55,582	318,442
2008–2009	281,485	35,077	316,562
2007–2008	276,314	82,151	358,465
2006–2007	234,420	53,594	288,014
2005–2006	204,548	42,487	247,035
2004–2005	188,004	50,193	238,197
2003–2004	174,611	32,727	207,338
2002–2003	153,336	24,153	177,489
2001–2002	151,405	24,154	175,559
2000–2001	171,320	53,740	225,060
1999–2000	175,196	57,799	232,995
1998–1999	176,783	39,332	216,115
1997–1998	204,408	76,818	281,226

[a]Original estimate

Government operating and capital revenue (as % of GDP)

	Operating revenue [as % of GDP]	*Capital revenue [as % of GDP]*	*Total government revenue [as % of GDP]*
2021–2022[a]	16.4	4.2	20.7
2020–2021	17.1	3.9	21.0
2019–2020	15.3	5.5	20.8
2018–2019	16.0	5.1	21.2
2017–2018	16.6	6.7	23.3
2016–2017	16.5	6.5	23.0
2015–2016	15.9	2.9	18.8
2014–2015	17.4	3.7	21.2
2013–2014	16.6	4.7	21.3

	Operating revenue [as % of GDP]	*Capital revenue [as % of GDP]*	*Total government revenue [as % of GDP]*
2012–2013	16.9	4.8	21.7
2011–2012	17.5	5.1	22.6
2010–2011	16.9	4.3	21.2
2009–2010	15.8	3.3	19.2
2008–2009	16.5	2.1	18.5
2007–2008	16.7	5.0	21.7
2006–2007	15.6	3.6	19.2
2005–2006	14.5	3.0	17.5
2004–2005	14.3	3.8	18.1
2003–2004	13.9	2.6	16.5
2002–2003	11.8	1.9	13.7
2001–2002	11.5	1.8	13.3
2000–2001	12.8	4.0	16.8
1999–2000	13.6	4.5	18.1
1998–1999	13.5	3.0	16.5
1997–1998	14.9	5.6	20.5

[a]Original estimate

Government revenue by major sources (in $ million)

	Profits tax [$ million]	*Salaries tax [$ million]*	*Land premium [$ million]*	*Stamp duties [$ million]*	*Investment income [$ million]*	*Other incomes [$ million]*	*Total government revenue [$ million]*
2021–2022[a]	126,650	64,390	97,600	92,000	84,578	125,887	591,105
2020–2021	135,540	75,027	88,713	89,045	52,426	123,479	564,230
2019–2020	155,900	50,412	141,728	67,198	48,399	127,289	590,926
2018–2019	166,620	60,146	116,861	79,979	40,342	135,826	599,774
2017–2018	139,100	60,839	164,811	95,173	21,443	138,471	619,837
2016–2017	139,238	59,077	127,970	61,899	20,725	164,215	573,124
2015–2016	140,227	57,868	60,893	62,680	183	128,156	450,007
2014–2015	137,847	59,347	77,804	74,845	215	128,610	478,668
2013–2014	120,882	55,620	84,255	41,515	37,000	116,074	455,346
2012–2013	125,638	50,467	69,563	42,880	37,995	115,607	442,150
2011–2012	118,600	51,761	84,644	44,356	37,246	101,116	437,723
2010–2011	93,183	44,255	65,545	51,005	33,933	88,560	376,481
2009–2010	76,605	41,245	39,632	42,383	33,625	84,952	318,442
2008–2009	104,151	39,008	16,936	32,162	46,571	77,734	316,562
2007–2008	91,423	37,479	62,318	51,549	27,920	87,776	358,465
2006–2007	71,919	38,586	37,001	25,077	29,418	86,013	288,014
2005–2006	69,797	37,494	29,472	17,867	10,372	82,033	247,035
2004–2005	58,640	33,990	32,033	15,851	14,674	83,009	238,197
2003–2004	48,770	27,977	5415	11,246	25,895	88,035	207,338
2002–2003	38,799	29,733	11,476	7458	17,550	72,473	177,489

	Profits tax [$ million]	*Salaries tax [$ million]*	*Land premium [$ million]*	*Stamp duties [$ million]*	*Investment income [$ million]*	*Other incomes [$ million]*	*Total government revenue [$ million]*
2001–2002	44,376	28,634	10,327	8637	872	82,713	175,559
2000–2001	42,969	26,303	29,531	10,911	23,519	91,827	225,060
1999–2000	37,699	24,831	34,810	12,116	41,920	81,619	232,995
1998–1999	45,252	25,063	19,251	10,189	39,325	77,035	216,115
1997–1998	55,347	30,159	62,481	29,097	17,925	86,217	281,226

[a]Original estimate

Government revenue by major sources (as % of GDP)

	Profits tax [as % of GDP]	*Salaries tax [as % of GDP]*	*Land premium [as % of GDP]*	*Stamp duties [as % of GDP]*	*Investment income [as % of GDP]*	*Other incomes [as % of GDP]*	*Total government revenue [as % of GDP]*
2021–2022[a]	4.4	2.3	3.4	3.2	3.0	4.4	20.7
2020–2021	5.0	2.8	3.3	3.3	1.9	4.6	21.0
2019–2020	5.5	1.8	5.0	2.4	1.7	4.5	20.8
2018–2019	5.9	2.1	4.1	2.8	1.4	4.8	21.2
2017–2018	5.2	2.3	6.2	3.6	0.8	5.2	23.3
2016–2017	5.6	2.4	5.1	2.5	0.8	6.6	23.0
2015–2016	5.8	2.4	2.5	2.6	0.0	5.3	18.8
2014–2015	6.1	2.6	3.4	3.3	0.0	5.7	21.2
2013–2014	5.7	2.6	3.9	1.9	1.7	5.4	21.3
2012–2013	6.2	2.5	3.4	2.1	1.9	5.7	21.7
2011–2012	6.1	2.7	4.4	2.3	1.9	5.2	22.6
2010–2011	5.2	2.5	3.7	2.9	1.9	5.0	21.2
2009–2010	4.6	2.5	2.4	2.6	2.0	5.1	19.2
2008–2009	6.1	2.3	1.0	1.9	2.7	4.5	18.5
2007–2008	5.5	2.3	3.8	3.1	1.7	5.3	21.7
2006–2007	4.8	2.6	2.5	1.7	2.0	5.6	19.2
2005–2006	4.9	2.7	2.1	1.3	0.7	5.8	17.5
2004–2005	4.5	2.6	2.4	1.2	1.1	6.3	18.1
2003–2004	3.9	2.2	0.4	0.9	2.1	7.0	16.5
2002–2003	3.0	2.3	0.9	0.6	1.4	5.5	13.7
2001–2002	3.4	2.2	0.8	0.7	0.1	6.1	13.3
2000–2001	3.2	2.0	2.2	0.8	1.8	6.8	16.8
1999–2000	2.9	1.9	2.7	0.9	3.3	6.4	18.1
1998–1999	3.5	1.9	1.5	0.8	3.0	5.8	16.5
1997–1998	4.0	2.2	4.6	2.1	1.3	6.3	20.5

[a]Original estimate

Government operating and capital expenditure (in $ million)

	Operating expenditure			*Capital expenditure [$ million]*	*Total government expenditure [$ million]*
	Recurrent expenditure [$ million]	*Non-recurrent expenditure [$ million]*	*Total operating expenditure [$ million]*		
2021–2022[a]	517,624	94,276	611,900	115,927	727,827
2020–2021	467,094	251,950	719,044	97,022	816,066
2019–2020	438,760	84,451	523,211	84,619	607,830
2018–2019	402,990	29,455	432,445	99,380	531,825
2017–2018	361,812	9085	370,897	99,966	470,863
2016–2017	344,638	8618	353,256	108,796	462,052
2015–2016	324,532	22,833	347,365	88,268	435,633
2014–2015	305,090	11,227	316,317	79,866	396,183
2013–2014	284,389	53,325	337,714	95,829	433,543
2012–2013	262,321	40,621	302,942	74,382	377,324
2011–2012	242,496	53,950	296,446	67,591	364,037
2010–2011	223,173	16,120	239,293	62,067	301,360
2009–2010	221,180	13,187	234,367	54,658	289,025
2008–2009	214,119	43,888	258,007	54,405	312,412
2007–2008	199,446	5288	204,734	30,081	234,815
2006–2007	189,498	4475	193,973	32,890	226,863
2005–2006	187,162	5300	192,462	40,609	233,071
2004–2005	192,295	4611	196,906	45,329	242,235
2003–2004	197,291	5943	203,234	44,232	247,466
2002–2003	198,004	2306	200,310	38,867	239,177
2001–2002	195,592	3151	198,743	40,147	238,890
2000–2001	184,522	2164	186,686	46,207	232,893
1999–2000	173,913	2008	175,921	47,122	223,043
1998–1999	164,277	13,129	177,406	61,950	239,356
1997–1998	149,386	11,180	160,566	33,794	194,360

[a]Original estimate

Government operating and capital expenditure (in as % of GDP)

	Operating expenditure			*Capital expenditure [as % of GDP]*	*Total government expenditure [as % of GDP]*
	Recurrent expenditure [as % of GDP]	*Non-recurrent expenditure [as % of GDP]*	*Total operating expenditure [as % of GDP]*		
2021–2022[a]	18.1	3.3	21.4	4.1	25.5
2020–2021	17.4	9.4	26.7	3.6	30.4
2019–2020	15.4	3.0	18.4	3.0	21.4
2018–2019	14.2	1.0	15.3	3.5	18.8
2017–2018	13.6	0.3	13.9	3.8	17.7
2016–2017	13.8	0.3	14.2	4.4	18.6
2015–2016	13.5	1.0	14.5	3.7	18.2
2014–2015	13.5	0.5	14.0	3.5	17.5
2013–2014	13.3	2.5	15.8	4.5	20.3
2012–2013	12.9	2.0	14.9	3.7	18.5
2011–2012	12.5	2.8	15.3	3.5	18.8
2010–2011	12.6	0.9	13.5	3.5	17.0
2009–2010	13.3	0.8	14.1	3.3	17.4
2008–2009	12.5	2.6	15.1	3.2	18.3
2007–2008	12.1	0.3	12.4	1.8	14.2
2006–2007	12.6	0.3	12.9	2.2	15.1
2005–2006	13.3	0.4	13.6	2.9	16.5
2004–2005	14.6	0.4	15.0	3.4	18.4
2003–2004	15.7	0.5	16.2	3.5	19.7
2002–2003	15.3	0.2	15.4	3.0	18.4
2001–2002	14.8	0.2	15.0	3.0	18.1
2000–2001	13.8	0.2	14.0	3.5	17.4
1999–2000	13.5	0.2	13.7	3.7	17.3
1998–1999	12.6	1.0	13.6	4.7	18.3
1997–1998	10.9	0.8	11.7	2.5	14.2

[a]Original estimate

Recurrent expenditure by policy area group (in $ million)

	Education [$ million]	*Social welfare [$ million]*	*Health [$ million]*	*Others[a] [$ million]*	*Total recurrent expenditure [$ million]*
2021–2022[b]	100,710	105,689	95,943	215,282	517,624
2020–2021[c]	97,123	90,936	88,929	195,158	472,146
2019–2020	92,438	81,555	82,142	182,625	438,760
2018–2019	85,528	79,486	72,529	165,447	402,990
2017–2018	80,233	65,349	62,616	153,614	361,812

	Education [$ million]	*Social welfare [$ million]*	*Health [$ million]*	*Others[a] [$ million]*	*Total recurrent expenditure [$ million]*
2016–2017	75,533	63,548	58,712	146,845	344,638
2015–2016	72,352	58,265	56,473	137,442	324,532
2014–2015	67,803	54,285	54,091	128,911	305,090
2013–2014	63,458	51,635	49,890	119,406	284,389
2012–2013	60,449	42,813	46,226	112,833	262,321
2011–2012	55,526	40,333	41,491	105,146	242,496
2010–2011	51,034	37,577	36,774	97,788	223,173
2009–2010	50,831	39,405	35,333	95,611	221,180
2008–2009	49,863	38,511	33,849	91,896	214,119
2007–2008	46,794	33,979	31,641	87,032	199,446
2006–2007	44,602	32,424	29,830	82,642	189,498
2005–2006	44,527	31,989	29,286	81,360	187,162
2004–2005	45,116	31,910	30,136	85,133	192,295
2003–2004	47,203	31,917	31,650	86,521	197,291
2002–2003	47,775	30,802	32,323	87,104	198,004
2001–2002	47,023	28,594	31,930	88,045	195,592
2000–2001	45,030	27,025	30,479	81,988	184,522
1999–2000	43,627	26,376	29,880	74,030	173,913
1998–1999	41,614	24,906	28,762	68,995	164,277
1997–1998	37,325	19,962	26,005	66,094	149,386

[a]Covering security, infrastructure, economic, housing, environment and food, community and external affairs and support
[b]Original estimate
[c]RE: Revised estimate

Recurrent expenditure by policy area group (in as % of GDP)

	Education [as % of GDP]	*Social welfare [as % of GDP]*	*Health [as % of GDP]*	*Others[a] [as % of GDP]*	*Total recurrent expenditure [as % of GDP]*
2021–2022[b]	3.5	3.7	3.4	7.5	18.1
2020–2021[c]	3.6	3.4	3.3	7.3	17.6
2019–2020	3.2	2.9	2.9	6.4	15.4
2018–2019	3.0	2.8	2.6	5.8	14.2
2017–2018	3.0	2.5	2.4	5.8	13.6
2016–2017	3.0	2.6	2.4	5.9	13.8
2015–2016	3.0	2.4	2.4	5.7	13.5
2014–2015	3.0	2.4	2.4	5.7	13.5
2013–2014	3.0	2.4	2.3	5.6	13.3

	Education [as % of GDP]	*Social welfare [as % of GDP]*	*Health [as % of GDP]*	*Others[a] [as % of GDP]*	*Total recurrent expenditure [as % of GDP]*
2012–2013	3.0	2.1	2.3	5.5	12.9
2011–2012	2.9	2.1	2.1	5.4	12.5
2010–2011	2.9	2.1	2.1	5.5	12.6
2009–2010	3.1	2.4	2.1	5.7	13.3
2008–2009	2.9	2.3	2.0	5.3	12.5
2007–2008	2.8	2.1	1.9	5.3	12.1
2006–2007	3.0	2.2	2.0	5.4	12.6
2005–2006	3.2	2.3	2.1	5.7	13.3
2004–2005	3.4	2.4	2.3	6.5	14.6
2003–2004	3.8	2.5	2.5	6.9	15.7
2002–2003	3.7	2.4	2.5	6.7	15.3
2001–2002	3.6	2.2	2.4	6.6	14.8
2000–2001	3.4	2.0	2.3	6.1	13.8
1999–2000	3.4	2.1	2.3	5.7	13.5
1998–1999	3.2	1.9	2.2	5.3	12.6
1997–1998	2.7	1.5	1.9	4.8	10.9

[a]Covering security, infrastructure, economic, housing, environment and food, community and external affairs and support
[b]Original estimate
[c]RE: Revised estimate

Bibliography

Ackrén, M. (2009). *Conditions for Different Autonomy Regimes in the World: A Fuzzy-Set Application.* Åbo Akademi University Press.

Allen, R., Hemming, R., & Potter, B. H. (2013). Introduction: The Meaning, Content and Objectives of Public Financial Management. In R. Allen, R. Hemming, & B. H. Potter (Eds.), *The International Handbook of Public Financial Management* (pp. 1–12). Palgrave Macmillan.

Asher, M. G. (1989). Fiscal System and Practices in Singapore. In Mukul G. Asher (Ed.), *Fiscal System and Practices in ASEAN Countries* (pp. 131–83). Singapore: Institute of Southeast Asian Studies.

Asher, M. G., Bali, A. S., & Kwan, C. Y. (2015). Public Financial Management in Singapore: Key Characteristics and Prospects. *The Singapore Economic Review, 60*(03), 1550032–1550018.

Baumgartner Jones, B. D., Breunig, F. R., Wlezien, C., Soroka, C., Foucault, S., François, M., Green, A., Pedersen, C., Koski, C., John, P., et al. (2009). A General Empirical Law of Public Budgets: A Comparative Analysis. *American Journal of Political Science, 53*(4), 855–873. https://doi.org/10.1111/j.1540-5907.2009.00405.x.

Bland, R. (2007). *A Budgeting Guide for Local Government.* ICMA Press.

Blöchliger, H. (2005). *Fiscal Autonomy of Sub-Central Governments.* OECD Network on Fiscal Relations Across Governments Working Papers, No. 2. Paris: OECD.

Blöndal, J. R. (2006). Budgeting in Singapore. *OECD Journal on Budgeting, 6*(1), 45–86.

Branch, F. (1995). *Practitioner's Guide: Management of Public Finances.* Government Printer.

B. C. H. Fong, *Hong Kong Public Budgeting*, Hong Kong Studies Reader Series, https://doi.org/10.1007/978-981-16-5363-6

Brendon, P. (2007). *The Decline and Fall of the British Empire 1781–1997*. Jonathan Cape Bright.

Bush, R. C. (2016). *Hong Kong in the Shadow of China: Living with the Leviathan*. Brookings Institution Press.

Carothers, T. (2002). The End of the Transition Paradigm. *Journal of Democracy, 13*(1), 5–21.

Case, W. (2008). Hybrid Politics and New Competitiveness: Hong Kong's 2007 Chief Executive Election. *East Asia, 25*(4), 365–388.

Castells, A. (2014). Catalonia and Spain at the Crossroads: Financial and Economic Aspects. *Oxford Review of Economic Policy, 30*(2), 277–296.

Chan, E. Y. M. (2012). Civil Society. In W. M. Lam, P. L. T. Lui, & W. Wilson (Eds.), *Contemporary Hong Kong Government and Politics* (pp. 179–198). Hong Kong University Press.

Chan, J. M., & Lee, F. L. F. (2012). Mass Media and Public Opinion. In W. M. Lam, P. L. T. Lui, & W. Wilson (Eds.), *Contemporary Hong Kong Government and Politics* (pp. 233–246). Hong Kong University Press.

Chan, M. K., & Clark, D. J. (1991). Democracy Derailed: Realpolitik in the Making of the Hong Kong Basic Law, 1985–90. In M. K. Chan & D. J. Clark (Eds.), *The Hong Kong Basic Law: Blueprint for "Stability and Prosperity" Under Chinese Sovereignty?* (pp. 3–35). Hong Kong University Press.

Chan, W. Y., & Cheng, E. W. (2020). State-Society Relations in Hong Kong and Macau: A Historical Institutionalist Analysis. In M. U. Ieong (Ed.), *Macau 20 Years After the Handover: Changes and Challenges Under "One Country, Two Systems"* (pp. 121–134). Routledge.

Chang, S. H. (2010). *From Years Congress to Comprehensive Re-Election: One Aspect of the Democratization Process in Taiwan*. M.phil. Dissertation, National Chengchi University, Taiwan.

Cheung, A. B. L. (1998). The Transition of Bureaucratic Authority: The Political Role of the Senior Civil Service in the Post–1997 Governance of Hong Kong. In L. Pang-Kwong (Ed.), *Political Order and Power Transition in Hong Kong* (pp. 79–108). Chinese University Press.

Cheung, A. B. L. (2005). *Budgeting for Results or Budgeting for Politics: Budget Reforms, Fiscal Stability and Distributional Politics in Hong Kong Re-Examineds*. A Paper Presented in the 61st Congress of the International Institute of Public Finance Jeju, Korea, 22–25 August 2005.

Cheung, A. B. L. (2006). Budgetary Reforms in Two City States: Impact on the Central Budget Agency in Hong Kong and Singapore. *International Review of Administrative Sciences, 72*(3), 341–361.

Cheung, A. B. L. (2007). Executive-Led Governance or Executive Power 'Hollowed-Out' – The Political Quagmire of Hong Kong. *Asian Journal of Political Science, 15*(1), 17–38.

Chiu, H. (1994). Constitutional Development and Reform in the Republic of China on Taiwan. In B. Lin & J. T. Myers (Eds.), *Contemporary China and the Changing International Community* (pp. 3–34). University of South California.

Chiu, S., & Wong, V. (2005). Hong Kong: From Familistic to Confucian Welfare. In A. Walker & C. K. Wong (Eds.), *East Asian Welfare Regimes in Transition: From Confucianism to Globalisation* (pp. 95–117). Policy Press.

Chou, B. K. P. (2013). Elections in Hong Kong: International Perspectives and Implications for China. In P. E. Lam, Y. Qin, & M. Yang (Eds.), *China and East Asia: After the Wall Street Crisis* (Vol. 33, pp. 75–99). World Scientific Publishing.

Chu, Y. H., & Lin, J. W. (2001). Political Development in Twentieth-Century Taiwan: State-Building, Regime Transformation and the Construction of National Identity. In R. L. Edmonds & S. M. Goldstein (Eds.), *Taiwan in the Twentieth Century: A Retrospective View* (pp. 102–129). Cambridge University Press.

Colonial Office. (1843). *Rules and Regulations for Her Majesty's Colonial Service.* Printed by George E. Eyre and William Spottiswoode, Printers to the Queen's Most Excellent Majesty, for Her Majesty's Stationery Office.

Cooper, J. F. (1999). *Taiwan: Nation-State or Province?* (3rd ed.). Westview Press.

Cullen, R., & Wong, A. (2012). *The Foundations of the Hong Kong Revenue Regime.* Civic Exchange.

Dawn.com. (2003). World Economic Report. 8 September. Retrieved June 5, 2021, from https://www.dawn.com/news/114259/world-economic-report

Dayley, R. (2020). *Southeast Asia in the New International Era* (8th ed.). Routledge.

De Renzio, P., & Masud, H. (2011). Measuring and Promoting Budget Transparency: The Open Budget Index as a Research and Advocacy Tool. *Governance, S1*, 607–616.

Dollery, B., Kitchen, H., Mcmillan, M., & Shah, A. (2020). *Local Public, Fiscal and Financial Governance an International Perspective.* Palgrave Macmillan.

Drummond, P., & Mansoor, A. (2002). *Macroeconomic Management and the Devolution of Fiscal Powers.* IMF Working Paper 02/76, International Monetary Fund, Washington.

Economist Intelligence Unit. (2018). How to Take Advantage of a Huge Fiscal Surplus? February 28. Retrieved February 12, 2021, from http://country.eiu.com/article.aspx?articleid=896476473&country=hong+kong&topic=economy&subtopic=_4

Fell, D. (2018). *Government and Politics in Taiwan.* Routledge.

Fong, B. C. H. (2008). An Analysis of the 2003 'Zero-Three-Three' Civil Service Pay Reduction Settlement in Hong Kong: A Neopluralist Perspective. *Asian Profile, 36*(6), 559–580.

Fong, B. C. H. (2014). *Hong Kong's Governance Under Chinese Sovereignty: The Failure of the State-Business Alliance After 1997*. Routledge.

Fong, B. C. H. (2015). The Politics of Budget Surpluses: The Case of China's HKSAR. *International Review of Administrative Sciences, 81*(1), 134–157.

Fong, B. C. H. (2016). In-Between Liberal Authoritarianism and Electoral Authoritarianism: Hong Kong's Democratization Under Chinese Sovereignty, 1997–2016. *Democratization, 24*(4), 724–750.

Fong, B. C. H. (2018). Executive-Legislative Disconnection in the HKSAR: The Erosion of the Legislative Support Base of the Chief Executives, 1997–2017. In B. C. H. Fong & T. L. Lui (Eds.), *Hong Kong: 20 Years After the Handover – Emerging Social and Institutional Fractures After 1997* (pp. 45–71). Palgrave Macmillan.

Fong, B. C. H. (2019). Democratization and Budget Openness: Evidences from Hong Kong, Macao, and Taiwan. *International Review of Administrative Sciences*. Article First Published Online: 8 July 2019. https://doi.org/10.1177/0020852319845453

Fong, B. C. H. (2020). Practicing Autonomy Within a Communist State: Hong Kong's Autonomy from Handover to Anti-Extradition Bill Movement, 1997 to 2019. *Communist and Post-Communist Studies, 53*(4), 68–90.

Fong, B. C. H. (2021a). Deficit Politics and Surplus Politics: A Comparative Study of Hong Kong and Singapore. *International Public Management Journal*. Article First Published Online: 1 April 2021. https://doi.org/10.1080/10967494.2021.1903633

Fong, B. C. H. (2021b). Budget Oversight in Territorial Autonomies: A Comparative Analysis of Hong Kong and Macao. *International Review of Administrative Sciences*.

Fong, B. C. H., & Ichijo, A. (2022). *Routledge Handbook of Comparative Territorial Autonomies*. Routledge. [Forthcoming].

Gardner, L., & Roy, T. (2020). *The Economic History of Colonialism*. Bristol University Press.

Ghai, Y. (1999). *Hong Kong's New Constitutional Order: The Resumption of Chinese Sovereignty and the Basic Law*. Hong Kong University Press.

Ghai, Y. P., & Woodman, S. (2013). *Practising Self-Government: A Comparative Study of Autonomous Regions*. Cambridge University Press.

Giraud, O., & Maggetti, M. (2015). Methodological Pluralism. In D. Braun & M. Maggetti (Eds.), *Comparative Politics: Theoretical and Methodological Challenges* (pp. 90–124). Edward Elgar.

Glennerster, R., & Yongseok, S. (2008). Does Transparency Pay? *IMF Staff Papers, 55*(1), 183–209.

Gonçalves, A. M. A. (2009). Macau's Autonomy: Looking for a Fresh Awakening? In J. C. Oliveira & P. Cardinal (Eds.), *One Country, Two Systems, Three Legal Orders: Perspectives of Evolution, Essays on Macau's Legal Status After the Resumption of Sovereignty by China* (pp. 733–740). Springer.

Goodhart, C., & Dai, L. (2003). *Intervention to Save Hong Kong: The Authorities' Counter – Speculation in Financial Markets*. Oxford University Press.

Goodstadt, L. F. (2009). *Uneasy Partners: The Conflict Between Public Interest and Private Profit Interest in Hong Kong*. Hong Kong University Press.

Goodstadt, L. F. (2010). Fiscal Freedom and the Making of Hong Kong's Capitalist Society. *China Information, 24*(3), 273–294.

Greene, J. E. (2020). *Public Finance: An International Perspective*. Singapore: World Scientific Publishing Co.

Guess, G., & Leloup, L. (2010). *Comparative Public Budgeting: Global Perspectives on Taxing and Spending*. State University of New York Press.

Guiraudon, V. (2020). Methodological Pluralism in European Political Science. In B. Thibaud, I. Engeli, & D. Garzia (Eds.), *Political Science in Europe. Achievements, Challenges, Prospects* (pp. 63–82). ECPR Press.

Hague, R., & Harrop, M. (2013). *Comparative Government and Politics: An Introduction*. Palgrave Macmillan.

Hallerberg, M., Rolf, S., & Von Hagen, J. (2009). The Political Economy of Budget Deficits. In A. Ayuso-I-Casals, S. Deroose, E. Flores, & L. Moulin (Eds.), *Policy Instruments for Sound Fiscal Policies Fiscal Rules and Institutions* (pp. 127–148). Palgrave Macmillan.

Hameed, F. (2005). *Fiscal Transparency and Economic Outcomes*. IMF Working Paper (WP/05/225). Washington, International Monetary Fund.

Harris, P. (1988). *Hong Kong: A Study in Bureaucratic Politics*. Heinemann Asia.

Heald, D. (2012). Why is Transparency About Public Expenditure so Elusive? *International Review of Administrative Sciences, 78*(1), 30–49.

Hepburn, E., & Detterbeck, K. (2018). Introduction to the Handbook of Territorial Politics. In E. Hepburn & K. Detterbeck (Eds.), *Handbook of Territorial Politics* (pp. 1–14). Edward Elgar.

Hong Kong Special Administrative Region Government. (2002). Chief Executive's Remarks. Retrieved June 5, 2021, from https://www.info.gov.hk/gia/general/200212/07/1207155.htm

Hong Kong Special Administrative Region Government. (2003). Speech on the 2003–04 Budget delivered by the Financial Secretary. Retrieved June 5, 2021, from https://www.budget.gov.hk/2003/eng/budget.htm#The%20Size%20and%20Pay%20of%20the%20Civil%20Service

Hong Kong Special Administrative Region Government. (2011). Speech by the Financial Secretary on Second Reading Debate on Appropriation Bill 2011. Retrieved June 5, 2021, from http://www.info.gov.hk/gia/general/201104/13/p201104130221.htm

Hong Kong Special Administrative Region Government. (2013). Speech by the Financial Secretary on Second Reading Debate on Appropriation Bill 2013. Retrieved June 5, 2021, from http://www.info.gov.hk/gia/general/201302/27/p201302270241.htm

Hooghe, L., Marks, G., & Schakel, A. H. (2016). *Measuring Regional Authority.* Oxford University Press.

Ide, E., & Park, G. (2015). *Deficits and Debt in Industrialized Democracies.* Routledge.

Imbeau, L., & Pétry, F. (2004). The Political Economy of Public Deficits. In L. Imbeau & F. Pétry (Eds.), *Politics, Institutions, and Fiscal Policy: Deficits and Surpluses in Federated States* (pp. 1–19). Lexington Books.

Institute of Digital Government. (2017). *Waseda-IAC International Digital Government Ranking 2017 Report.* Tokyo, Japan. http://iacio.org/pdf/2017_digital-government_ranking_press_release.pdf

International Budget Partnership. (2016). *Guide to the Open Budget Questionnaire: An Explanation of the Questions and the Response Options.* Washington. https://www.internationalbudget.org/wp-content/uploads/open-budget-survey-2017-guide-andquestionnaire-english.pdf

International Budget Partnership. (2019). *Guide to the Open Budget Questionnaire: An Explanation of the Questions and the Response Options.* Washington, DC. Retrieved February 3, 2021, from https://www.internationalbudget.org/sites/default/files/2020-04/2019_Guide_and_Questionnaire_EN.pdf

International Budget Partnership. (2020). *Open Budget Survey 2019.* Washington, DC. Retrieved February 3, 2021, from https://www.internationalbudget.org/open-budget-survey/open-budget-survey-2019

International Budget Partnership. (2021). *About.* Washington, DC. Retrieved February 3, 2021, from https://www.internationalbudget.org/open-budget-survey/about

International Monetary Fund. (2020). *How the IMF is Promoting Transparent and Accountable Use of COVID-19 Financial Assistance.* Washington, DC. Retrieved February 3, 2021, from https://www.imf.org/en/about/factsheets/sheets/2020/04/30/how-imf-covid19-financial-help-is-used

Jansen, J. C., Osterhammel, J., & Riemer, J. (2017). *Decolonization: A Short History.* Princeton University Press.

Jensen, J. L., Mortensen, P. B., & Serritzlew, S. (2019). A Comparative Distributional Method for Public Administration Illustrated Using Public Budget Data. *Journal of Public Administration Research and Theory, 29*(3), 460–473. https://doi.org/10.1093/jopart/muy056.

Kaczorowska, A. (2010). *Public International Law* (4th edition). Abingdon: Routledge.

Kettl, D. F. (2003). *Deficit Politics: The Search for Balance in American Politics.* Longman.

Khagram, S., De Renzio, P., & Fung, A. (2013). Overview and Synthesis: The Political Economy of Fiscal Transparency, Participation, and Accountability Around the World. In S. Khagram, A. Fung, & P. De Renzio (Eds.), *Open Budgets: The Political Economy of Transparency, Participation, and Accountability* (pp. 1–50). Project MUSE.

Khan, A. (2019). *Fundamentals of Public Budgeting and Finance*. Springer Nature.

Kwong, Y. H. (2017). Ruling Coalition Restructuring under Macao's Hybrid Regime. *China Review, 173*(3), 111–139.

Kwong, Y. H., & Wong, M. Y. H. (2017). State Size and Democratization in Hybrid Regimes: The Chinese Island Cities of Macau and Hong Kong. *Island Studies Journal, 12*(2), 113–126.

Lam, J. (2002). Globalization and Fiscal Management in Hong Kong. *New Zealand Journal of Asian Studies, 4*(1), 62–83.

Lasater, M. L. (1990). *A Step Toward Democracy – The December 1989 Election in Taiwan, ROC*. AEI Press.

Lau, S. K. (1982). *Society and Politics in Hong Kong*. Chinese University Press.

Lee, R. D., Johnson, R. W., & Joyce, P. B. (2013). *Public Budgeting Systems* (9th ed.). Jones & Bartlett Learning.

Levine, P. (2013). *The British Empire Sunrise to Sunset* (2nd ed.). Pearson Education.

Littlewood, M. (2010). *Taxation Without Representation: The History of Hong Kong's Troublingly Successful Tax System*. Hong Kong University Press.

Liu, Z., & Su, Z. (2013). *Aomen Yu Xianggang Cai Zheng Zheng Ce Bi Jiao Yan Jiu [澳門與香港財政政策比較研究]*. Aomen Jing Ji Xue Hui (In Chinese).

Lo, C. S. S. (1990). *Public Budgeting in Hong Kong: An Incremental Decision-Making Approach*. Writers' and Publishers' Cooperative.

Lo, S. S. H. (2008). *Political Change in Macau*. Routledge.

Lo, S. S. H. (2020). *Casino Capitalism, Society and Politics in China's Macau*. Cambridge Scholars Publishing.

Lynch, T. D., & Martin, L. (1993). *Handbook of Comparative Public Budgeting and Financial Management*. Marcel Dekker.

Ma, N. (2007). *Political Development in Hong Kong: State, Political Society and Civil Society*. Hong Kong University Press.

Ma, N. (2012). Political Parties and Elections. In W. M. Lam, P. L. T. Lui, & W. Wong (Eds.), *Contemporary Hong Kong Government and Politics* (pp. 159–177). Hong Kong University Press.

Ma, N. (2020). China's Influence on Hong Kong's Elections: Evidence from Legislative Council Elections. In B. C. H. Fong, J. M. Wu, & A. J. Nathan (Eds.), *China's Influence and the Center-Periphery Tug of War in Hong Kong, Taiwan and Indo-Pacific* (pp. 91–104). Routledge.

Marquand, D. (2008). *Britain Since 1918: The Strange Career of British Democracy*. Weidenfeld & Nicolson.

Menifield, C. (2011). *Comparative Public Budgeting: A Global Perspective*. Jones & Bartlett Learning.

Merkel, W. (2011). Transition. In B. Badie, D. Berg-Schlosser, & L. Morlino (Eds.), *International Encyclopedia of Political Science* (pp. 2661–2663). SAGE Publications.

Miners, N. (1998). *The Government and Politics of Hong Kong* (5th ed.). Oxford University Press.

Morgan, I. W. (2009). *The Age of Deficits: Presidents and Unbalanced Budgets from Jimmy Carter to George W. Bush.* University Press of Kansas.

Nice, D. (2002). *Public Budgeting.* Wadsworth.

Oehl, B., Schaffer, L. M., & Bernauer, T. (2016). How to Measure Public Demand for Policies when There is No Appropriate Survey Data? *Journal of Public Policy, 37*(2), 1–32.

Orenstein, M. A., & Schmitz, H. P. (2006). The New Transnationalism and Comparative Politics. *Comparative Politics, 38*(4), 479–500.

Organization for Economic Co-Operation and Development. (2020). *Legislative Budget Oversight of Emergency Responses: Experiences During the Coronavirus (COVID 19) Pandemic.* Paris. Retrieved February 3, 2021, from https://www.oecd.org/coronavirus/policy-responses/legislative-budget-oversight-of-emergency-responses-experiences-during-the-coronavirus-covid-19-pandemic-ba4f2ab5

Ott, A. (1993). *Public Sector Budgets: A Comparative Study.* E. Elgar Pub.

Peters, B. G. (2013). *Strategies for Comparative Research in Political Science.* Palgrave Macmillan.

Ping, A. L. S. (2011). Challenges and Threats to Traditional Associations. In N. M. Lam & I. Scott (Eds.), *Gaming, Governance and Public Policy in Macao* (pp. 75–88). Hong Kong University Press.

Pola, G. (2016). *Principles and Practices of Fiscal Autonomy: Experiences, Debates and Prospects.* Routledge.

Posner, P. L. (2013). *The Politics of Fiscal Austerity: Democracies and Hard Choices.* OECD Publishing.

Rabushka, A. (1976). *Value for Money: The Hong Kong Budgetary Process.* Hoover Institution Press.

Rabushka, A. (1979). *Hong Kong: A Study in Economic Freedom.* University of Chicago Press.

Raudla, R. (2014). Budgetary Institutions. In J. Backhaus (Ed.), *Encyclopedia of Law and Economics* (pp. 1–9). Springer.

Reinikka, R., & Jakob, S. (2004). *The Power of Information: Evidence from a Newspaper Campaign to Reduce Capture (Policy Research Working Paper 3239).* World Bank.

Ríosa, A. M., Benito, B., & Bastida, F. (2013). Determinants of Central Government Budget Disclosure: An International Comparative Analysis. *Journal of Comparative Policy Analysis: Research and Practice, 15*(3), 235–254.

Ross, M. (2011). *Mineral wealth and budget transparency.* IBP Working Paper 2. Washington, International Budget Partnership.

Rubin, I. (1998). *Class, Tax, and Power Municipal Budgeting in the United States.* Chatham House.

Rubin, I. (2020). *The Politics of Public Budgeting: Getting and Spending, Borrowing and Balancing* (9th ed.). Sage/CQ Press.
Santiso, C. (2009). *The Political Economy of Government Auditing: Financial Governance and the Rule of Law in Latin America and Beyond*. Routledge.
Savage, J. D. (2015). Budgeting: Political Science Aspects. In J. D. Wright (Ed.), *International Encyclopaedia of the Social & Behavioral Sciences* (2nd ed., pp. 901–905). Elsevier.
Schafferer, C. (2003). The Legislative Yuan Election, Taiwan 2001. *Electoral Studies, 22*(3), 532–537.
Schmitt, D. A. (2006). *The Bechuanaland Pioneers and Gunners*. Praeger.
Schmitter, P. C., & Karl, T. L. (1991). What Democracy is … and is Not. *Journal of Democracy, 2*(3), 75–88.
Scott, I. (1989). *Political Change and the Crisis of Legitimacy in Hong Kong*. Oxford University Press.
Scott, I. (2010). *The Public Sector in Hong Kong*. Hong Kong University Press.
Seifert, J., Carlitz, R., & Mondo, E. (2013). The Open Budget Index (OBS) as a Comparative Statistical Tool. *Journal of Comparative Policy Analysis: Research and Practice, 15*(1), 87–101.
Shah, A. (2007). *Local Budgeting*. World Bank.
Share, C. (2007). *Where Empires Collided: Russian and Soviet Relations with Hong Kong, Taiwan, and Macao*. The Chinese University of Hong Kong Press.
South China Morning Post. (2011). Welfare Body Urges Long-Term Help for Needy. 14 February.
South China Morning Post. (2013). Legislators Want Tsang to Start Spending. 4 March.
Su, T. T. (2018). Public Budgeting System in Taiwan: Does it Lead to Better Value for Money? In A. Podger, T. T. Su, & J. Wanna (Eds.), *Value for Money: Budget and Financial Management Reform in the People's Republic of China* (pp. 79–93). Australian National University.
Sugimoto, I., & Tan, E. C. (2011). Government Fiscal Behaviour and Economic Growth of Singapore in the Twentieth Century. *The Singapore Economic Review, 56*(1), 19–40.
Sung, Y. W., & Lee, M. K. (1991). *The Other Hong Kong Report*. Chinese University Press.
Tang, S. H. (1989). *Fiscal Constitution and the Basic Law (Draft) of Hong Kong (BRC Working Papers Series; ES 89005)*. Business Research Centre, Hong Kong Baptist College.
Tang, S. H. (1991). *Hong Kong: 1991/92 Budget and the Long Term Financial Strategy (BRC Working Papers Series; ES 91016)*. Business Research Centre, Hong Kong Baptist College.
Tang, S. H. (1993). *Fiscal Legislation and Financial Control in Hong Kong (BRC Working Papers Series; ES 92031)*. Business Research Centre, Hong Kong Baptist College.

Tang, S. H. (1997). Budgetary Guidelines and Fiscal Performance in Hong Kong. *International Journal of Public Sector Management, 10*(7), 547–571.

The Standard. (2011a). Miserly – That's How Legislators Describe It. 24 February.

The Standard. (2011b). Budget Cuts Popularity. 1 March.

The Standard. (2011c). $6,000 Cash in Hand. 3 March.

The Straits Times. (2015). Budget 2015: In Deficit, Yet Very Prudent at Heart. March 7. Retrieved February 12, 2021, from https://www.straitstimes.com/opinion/budget-2015-in-deficit-yet-very-prudent-at-heart

Thompson, F., Pierson, K., Hand, M. L., & Dothan, M. U. (2017). Is a Good Normative Model of Public Spending Run Backward a Good Positive Model? *Public Budgeting & Finance, 37*(2), 35–57. https://doi.org/10.1111/pbaf.12121

Thurmaier, K., & Willoughby, K. (2001). *Policy and Politics in State Budgeting*. M.E. Sharpe.

United Nations for Human Rights Office of the High Commissioner. (2017). *Realizing Human Rights Through Government Budgets*. New York: United Nations.

Ure, G. (2012). *Governors, Politics, and the Colonial Office: Public Policy in Hong Kong, 1918–58*. Hong Kong University Press.

Von Hagen, J. (2007). Budgeting Institutions for better Fiscal Performance. In A. Shah (Ed.), *Budgeting and Budgetary Institutions* (pp. 27–51). World Bank.

Wang, X. H. (2014). *Financial Management in the Public Sector: Tools, Applications, and Cases* (3rd ed.). M.E. Sharpe, Inc.

Warner, R. (2018). *Making the Most of the Budget Cycle: The Budget Oversight Stage*. International Budget Partnership: Open Budgets Blog. Retrieved February 3, 2021, from https://www.internationalbudget.org/2018/04/making-budget-cycle-budget-oversight-stage

Wehner, J. (2006). Assessing the Power of the Purse: An Index of Legislative Budget Institutions. *Political Studies, 54*(4), 767–785.

Wehner, J., & De Renzio, P. (2013). Citizens, Legislators, and Executive Disclosure: The Political Determinants of Fiscal Transparency. *World Development, 41*, 96–108.

Weller, M., & Katherine, N. (Eds.). (2010). *Asymmetric Autonomy and the Settlement of Ethnic Conflicts*. University of Pennsylvania Press.

Wildavsky, A. B. (1986). *Budgeting: A Comparative Theory of the Budgeting Process*. Transaction Publishers.

Wildavsky, A. B. (2004). *The New Politics of the Budgetary Process*. Pearson/Longman.

Wimmer, A., & Glick Schiller, N. (2002). Methodological Nationalism and Beyond: Nation-State Building, Migration and the Social Sciences. *Global Networks, 2*(4), 301–334.

Wong, W. (2009). The Days After the End of the Asian Miracle: The Budget Crisis of Hong Kong. In S. Ming (Ed.), *Politics and Government in Hong Kong: Crisis Under Chinese Sovereignty* (pp. 136–161). Routledge.

Woo, J. J. (2007). *3-In-1: Governing a Global Financial Centre*. World Scientific.

Yamamoto, K. (2018). Budgeting and Decision-Making. In A. Farazmand (Ed.), *Global Encyclopedia of Public Administration, Public Policy, and Governance* (pp. 476–483). Springer Nature.

Yu, E. W. Y. (2011). Executive-Legislature Relationships and the Development of Public Policy. In L. Newman & I. Scott (Eds.), *Gaming, Governance and Public Policy in Macao* (pp. 57–64). Hong Kong University Press.

Yu, G. (2015). *Hong Kong's Legislature Under China's Sovereignty, 1998–2013*. Brill Nijhoff.

Zheng, V., & Wan, P. S. (2014). *Gambling Dynamism: The Macao Miracle*. Springer.

The manufacturer's authorised representative in the EU is Springer Nature Customer Service Centre GmbH, Europaplatz 3, 69115 Heidelberg, Germany. If you have any concerns regarding our products, please contact ProductSafety@springernature.com

Printed and bound by CPI Group (UK) Ltd, Croydon, CR0 4YY
30/09/2026
02225514-0018